A FEAST
OF TRUE
FANDANGLES

Also available in Crescent

Dear Stranger
The Hour Before Midnight
It's Been a Lot of Fun
The Still Storm
The Falklands Whale
Deathwatch
Shattered
The Wrong Face
Love Child
The Gironde Incident
The House on Prague Street
The Stratford Story
A Presence in an Empty Room
I Sent a Letter to My Love
Outrage
Phoenix Rising
Delilah's Fortune
None Shall Spurn
Mysterious Railway Stories

Death Mail
Season of Change
The Cold Room
The Whitehall Sanction
Minnie Ashe at War
The Breadwinner
Incidental Music
The Domino Vendetta
Never Forgive, Never Forget
King's Wench
It's a Funny Game
Uninvited: The Visitation
Golgotha
Spring at Brookfield
Something Special
The Grand Order of Water Rats
The Queen and the Welshman
Slaughter Horse
Yesterday When I Was Young

A FEAST
OF TRUE
FANDANGLES

Patrick Campbell

A CRESCENT BOOK

To Vivienne and Irene

Copyright © Patrick Campbell, 1979
First published in Great Britain by
W. H. Allen & Co. Ltd, 1979
This Crescent edition published 1986

Set by Galleon Photosetting
Printed and bound in Great Britain by
The Garden City Press Ltd, Letchworth, Herts
for the publishers, W. H. Allen & Co. Plc
44 Hill Street, London W1X 8LB

All the articles included in this book have been previously published in
the *Sunday Times* between 1972 and 1979

British Library Cataloguing in Publication Data

Campbell, Patrick, *1911–*
A feast of true fandangles.
I. Title
828′.91407   PR6013.L43
ISBN 1-85188-056-9

Contents

Some others and I

At home abroad

All over the place

The little outdoors

At life's door

Some Others and I

Trying to work at work

Striking looks as though it has become exceedingly hard work.

In the old days, of course, it was simplicity itself. All you had to do was throw down your shovel and wait outside the gate until the gaffer told you you'd got the sack or the required 9d extra per week.

Now, on the other hand, you've got to be a professional striker, first of all to know what you're striking about – would it be a weighting allowance plus basic pay for overtime availability? – and then if you decide to strike how to go about the striking itself. Do you try to hammer the ears off the police or some of your own brothers? Or simply stand about in non-militant provocative attitudes until someone strikes you, putting you totally, basically and irrevocably in an on-going power situation?

With all this difficult work to be done strikers can certainly be excused for forgetting that what they are doing may well inconvenience, to the point of homicidal mania, millions of other people who are merely trying to work at work, but surely

3

from time to time it might not be presumptuous to remind them of our portion.

Thanks, for instance, to the differences between the BBC and the Association of Broadcasting Staff I slid down the hill to Nice Airport in a heavy snowfall on Friday the thirteenth – always a cheery day – to fly to London to record four programmes of *Call My Bluff* without knowing what was going to happen when I got there, due to a mass meeting of the ABS called for that very afternoon.

On arrival in London I nipped out to buy the packet of Bisto commissioned by Madame and got back to my lodgings in time to receive a call from our producer to the effect that we had been struck out of bounds, so severely that no recordings would be made that weekend.

I made a beeline for our travel agent several miles away to get my return ticket endorsed for Saturday instead of Monday, only to find that my ticket would be invalid unless I stayed in London for at least three nights. So, for only £83.50, I bought a single ticket for Nice. I could have saved myself the cab fare to the agency and back because, of course, I could have bought this ticket at Heathrow, but what with the ABS strike and snow and Friday the thirteenth and the packet of Bisto I was running a little off balance.

Before retiring that night I computerized my mind into awakening at 7.30 the following morning, to be in time for the car arriving at 8.30 to take me to the airport, and woke on the very dot of eight. Scrambling packing, shaving, with the ingestion of a slice of dry bread, all combined with a call to the car-hire firm to make sure they were coming. The phone rang for a curiously long time. Then a faint and somehow ragged voice said, ''Es?' It 'ent on to assure me, ever more faintly, that the car would be there. I looked at my watch again and saw that it wasn't 8.15. It was 4.15. No wonder the voice at the other end had been faint. I went back to bed and read a book until 7.30, when I began the day all over again with a more substantial breakfast.

When the car came I begged the driver to give my abject apologies to his boss. 'That's not my boss,' he said. 'That's my partner, Ted. He's recovering from a very serious operation.' Without, I reflected, much assistance from me.

As we took off from Heathrow, I opened the paper, glad to leave all this shame and confusion behind, and saw that the BBC strike had been settled the previous night. I spent the flight leaning forward, urging Air France to greater speed, knowing I'd be able to get back from Nice to London with British Airways by 4.15 p.m., almost exactly twelve hours since I'd got up. Over St Raphael I was flung back into my seat by a sudden thunderstorm which bounced us around like anything. A flash of lightning actually struck the plane right under my seat but at least we'd got rid of Friday the thirteenth.

In Nice Airport I sped to the British Airways desk. Any calls from Madame or the BBC? Not a word. But they said I was lucky to be there because owing to the electrical storm Air France had almost been diverted to Marseille. Leaving me to get home by bus?

When I did get home I felt as if I'd been up for about three weeks, and looked it, too. But I was able to give Madame her packet of Bisto, for which I had flown two thousand-odd miles.

I'm sure that the Association of Broadcasting Staff will regard this as adequate compensation for any trouble I might have been put to.

Thanks a million, lads. And here's to the next time.

Passportery

Madame's passport is about to die after ten years of pure and active life. To be without a passport is like having every drop of blood drained from the body. Therefore, the last time we were in London, she set off to get a new one, a deadly chore that would probably take as much as a couple of hours.

She came back surprisingly quickly with four photographs, a sheaf of forms and a newly-hardened attitude towards the Passport Office.

'I am informed,' she told me, 'that it will take from five to six weeks to provide me with a new passport, although it is impossible to imagine what they would be doing with my old one for the best part of two months.'

I voiced, not for the first time, an opinion I had held about the renewal of passports ever since the subject had come up. 'I cannot believe,' I said, 'that just because your passport is ten years old, in prime condition, with a pretty picture and an absolutely accurate record of your vital statistics—'

'No advance is made by saying that again.'

'That you've got to get a new one and it's going to take five or six weeks.' I reminded her, perhaps unnecessarily, of the time my passport had been dissolved, in my luggage, by the breaking of a bottle of presentation twelve-year-old Irish, and of how I'd got a new one in about twenty minutes from our Embassy in London.

'That's only an Irish passport,' she said.

We'd got back to a situation in which we had already spent many hours. 'All right, then,' I said, 'let's have a look at all those documents.' I was sure that buried in one of them must be a method of speeding up the renewal process.

'By all means,' she said generously. 'Try

7

From P2(C) to begin with.'

Form P2(C) was headed:

IMMIGRATION ACT 1971
INDICATION OF THE RIGHT OF ABODE IN
THE UNITED KINGDOM (PATRIALITY) IN
UNITED KINGDOM PASSPORTS ISSUED ON
OR AFTER JANUARY, 1973.

I got that instant contraction of the brain that reading any form gives everyone. 'What's patriality?' I said. I'd never even heard of it. An entirely new word had broken out in passportery.

'I cannot help you there,' Madame said. 'It has not yet arrived in the *Concise Oxford Dictionary, Second Edition*, 1929.'

'It better hurry up. How can you have patriality *in* United Kingdom passports?'

'What you want *in* your United Kingdom passport is obviously the indication of the right of abode in the United Kingdom. Or patriality.'

I reflected for quite some time. 'It seems to me,' I said, 'that the purpose of Form P2(C) is either to placate, or enrage, Mr Enoch Powell.'

'If we begin talking about Enoch Powell,' she said, 'my passport is going to run out long before I can get another one.'

So we brought all the documents back to France, and she began all over again with the British Consulate in Marseille, two hundred miles farther away from us than the one in Nice, which has been closed down in the

8

interests of economy. They provided her with another form or, rather, a roneoed sheet of paper. This requested her to send her previous passport with 'two identical full face black and white photographs, which must be NOT SMALLER THAN 2 ins × 1½ ins (50 × 38 mm) and UNGLAZED ON THE BACK. Polaroid and machine (photomaton) photographs are only acceptable if imprinted with PMI or PHOTOQUICK PASSPORTS. Colour photographs are only acceptable if imprinted with P/108, or KODAK PRINT, or AGFA-GEVAERT RVC'.

We looked at one another with sodden surmise. Then we looked at the photographs she had had taken, at some fair expense, in London. A speaking likeness, with no trace of the maniacal tendencies so often revealed by passport pictures. Size about right, after careful measurement, but undeniably a bit shiny – or GLAZED – on the back. And, of course, no sign of an imprint of PMI or PHOTOQUICK PASSPORTS. Clearly, some new photographs were required, so we drove to Grasse in eternal, torrential rain, new ones were taken and instructions given to come back for them in four days' time.

Madame spent the four days in filling up Form C1, and finding that one of the photographs should be endorsed by an MP, a JP, a Minister of Religion, Doctor, Lawyer, Bank Officer, Police Officer or a person of similar standing. The only person we could think of who was still standing was ex-headmaster Bayliss, so he came round and obliged.

It is noteworthy that Madame, in her new pix, seems to have had a slight stroke.

Not surprising, really.

The everything bowl

Coincidentally with casting an eye over a smallish advertisement for something called 'The Everything Bowl' in one of those American magazines that cater for the creature comforts, in spades, of millionaires – no particular nationality preferred – I broke the third of our all-American, multi-sprocket, fully automatic corkscrews, purchased in Los Angeles only eighteen months ago, although it would be fairer – to me – to say that the corkscrew broke itself.

It, like its precursors, was one of those corkscrews with two arms, like wings, sticking out, which rise into the air when what we call 'the collar' is screwed down on to the neck of the bottle. All we do then is to press the wings down again beside the body of the machine, thereby drawing the cork out of the bottle, more often than not, the effort leaving the cork puller panting only very slightly for two or three minutes, after the operation.

10

Until, that is, the two slender metal bars that keep the collar in place break off, doing in the multi-sprocket, fully automatic aspect of the tool which can nonetheless be used for its set purpose if the cork puller wears a reinforced boiler-maker's glove, in preference to laceration of the palm of the hand.

This third metal bar collapse, in only eighteen months, led me to have my first close look at this weighty, gleaming, even formidable all-American corkscrew, surely the very last thing in its field seeing that rich Americans go about drinking at home with a tool-kit that would outdo the primitive instruments of a brain surgeon. Along the top of this all-American super corkscrew, faintly embossed in miniature letters, ran the legend: 'Made In Italy'.

It was this revolting discovery that made me read the smallish advertisement for 'The Everything Bowl', absolutely word by word, with the help of a magnifying glass, in case further hanky-panky might be afoot, only to find something even more curious than an Italian-made all-American corkscrew.

In American hard-sell terms we began fairly gently:

AT LAST – A bowl big enough to be really useful!

My anti-purchase suspicion hackles rose perceptibly. Just a minute, I thought shrewdly. How big does a big enough bowl have to be to be really useful – for what?

The advertisers, obviously accustomed to this mulish opposition, sought to smooth me down. *'This thirteen quart beauty . . . heavy gauge stainless steel . . . perfectly proportioned for a variety of uses . . .'*

I took a short rest. Thirteen quarts! That must be about twenty-six pints. Enough celebratory drinks for a Rugger team, five refs and some linesmen. But what did our American cousins propose as a use for this enormous bucket?

Of course – enormous American cooking.

'Toss and serve large salads. Mix stuffing, large batches of cookies, pie fillings, make bread dough . . .'

With spades and pick-axes, stuffing albatrosses, the equivalent of twenty-six pints of buns, with one thousand friends round for lunch and three tons of leftovers. An essential utensil for every competent hostess—

But suddenly, at the very end of the advertisement, a sting in the tail as venomous as an all-American corkscrew made in Italy.

Bathe baby, soak feet, wash socks, bob for apples, catch drips, etc., etc., etc.

There it was, the ultimate hanky-panky. Wash your socks, in preparation for the coming party, hang 'em up on the line, give your Everything Bowl a swill around, begin to make your pie fillings, notice that Baby Junior's looking a bit grubby, begin again by giving him a bit of a splosh around, keeping the pie fillings to one side, hang him up

12

beside your socks, decide you might as well make the pie fillings into bread dough, moisten with a gallon of water from the leak in the kitchen roof . . .

A veritable maelstrom of frantic activity, all based upon one single bowl. And still the problem of where to put it, when Baby is clean and the gargantuan meal has been guzzled and someone has done something about the leak in the kitchen ceiling. Under the bed?

Progress really leaves us seniors groping back into the past, when tools were simple and fulfilled only their designed purpose and, if we get as far back as prehistoric times, made exclusively by ourselves, rather than in Italy or by more distant tribes fifty-two times bigger than us.

Not to be found a pitifully nostalgic, crippled old wool-gatherer, however, I offer you a brand-new tool. It's called 'The All Tool'. It's a plank thirty feet long, polished on one side, rough on the other, with a spoon at one end and a folding corkscrew at the other.

You'll love it, once you've got the hang of it.

Road show

This bright blue open lorry, laden with all this indescribable junk and towing the huge, rectangular yellow box pulled up in the space below the house and the two lads in the overalls jumped out and removed a large piece of our neighbour's fence in a matter of minutes.

I saw all this from the kitchen window so I was into the sitting-room in a flash, a post from which I can get a clear view of both sides of the road, right down to the corner where a clump of trees gets in my way.

I put it down to a pumping out of the soak-away. We all have private drainage arrangements round here and after heavy rain we get it round the ankles. On the other hand, the huge yellow box didn't look much like a receptacle for surplus sewage, and the junk in the back of the lorry seemed to be too complicated to be a mere pump. There seemed to be rubber tyres in there, a mass of pipes, iron beams, all sorts of stuff plastered with mud.

The overalled lads' next move amazed me. They detached their yellow box, drove the lorry right up against the hole they'd made in the fence and began to drag the wheeled junk into our neighbour's garden. In about twenty minutes they'd got the single front wheel of the junk stuck deeply in the mud in the garden, with the two back wheels still in the lorry, with the result that the lorry, thus attached to *terra firma*, immovably blocked the lane. And just at the time that the Mummies were coming down from the hills above to pick up their children from school, and the Daddies were coming home, up the hill, after a tiring day in the office. In no time at all we had five cars on one side of the lorry and six on the other. Very quickly I got myself a drink and put my armchair in the window. Obviously, spectacular viewing was in store.

Turned out to be first-class material. Everyone shouting, Mummies and Daddies trying to change cars, more shouting when they found they couldn't turn round, eventually two Daddies in good business suits climbing into the lorry, pushing the huge iron lump right into the garden, the lorry being backed out of the way and a grand finale of fourteen cars trying to get past one another with less than an inch to spare. I hadn't felt as tired in years, and turned in early.

Next morning, 7.30 a.m., still dark, I was plucked out of sleep by the thunderous roar of an engine. Sprang to the window and there below me was the scene incredibly changed.

The presumed yellow sewage disposal tank transformed into a bellowing diesel compressor. And in the garden the alleged pump presented itself, in the thin light of dawn, as a miniature oil derrick, with a long upright shaft with a mechanism attached to it, sprouting pipes and grinding a thick iron bar slowly into the ground. Oil! Our neighbour had struck oil! Perhaps we were sitting on it, too! All millionaires, for miles round. My word.

Roughly shaven, hastily dressed, I was at my viewing post in a matter of minutes, chewing blackened toast, sucking lukewarm coffee – and looking at the notice on the side of the van which had replaced the blue lorry. These lads weren't oil prospectors. They were water seekers and well-borers. Our neighbour, as sagacious as ever, had hit upon a method of dodging prohibitive water bills, and the rigours of summer drought. Well, Lord above, whatever next?

Apart from the hissing, roaring pandemonium Saturday was great fun. At one moment the hose blew off the compressor, releasing a blast of air that uprooted two bushes on the other side of the road and plastered them against our neighbour's kitchen window. Shortly after it had been repaired the stern old lady with the difficult mauve woollen hat rode across the pipe on her mobilette and, almost disembowelled, zigzagged off round the corner with spidery legs in thick stockings waggled horizontally in the air.

16

We had Sunday off. But a special thrill on Monday, about mid-day. We struck yellow, liquid mud, erupting spasmodically from the bore hole. Never will I forget the sight of the mother and the middle-aged daughter coming round the corner at the bottom of the hill, talking simultaneously as they have done for years on their way down to do their shopping, and passing by the bore hole, still talking, with the yellow mud erupting a bare five seconds after they'd passed the danger zone. They neither heard it nor turned to look at it, being in discussion about the prohibitive price of spuds.

It was a pity. Almost anything could have delayed them. The daughter forgetting her handbag, the mother deciding to change her hat, albeit for the first time in seven years. And then the two of them walking straight into this blast of mud.

The staggering around, the scooping of mud from eyes and hair, the shrill denunciation of the man working the drill, playing his handles like a cinema organ with his back turned to the road.

It would have taken them a long time to attract his attention but, of course, once they'd got it, in this howling din, we would have had a splendid set-to.

Unfortunately, all that died out in anticlimax. The oblivious, talking ladies went their way, the driller failed to strike water and retired, leaving our neighbour to cover the hole with a concrete slab and to forget as much as possible about what had happened. Apart from the mud, high in the surrounding trees, nothing might have happened at all.

But then, shortly afterwards, as reliably as a repertory company, Fate put on another show right in the middle of the road on an exact level with the mud-slinging gala, possibly having a strong plot-connection with it. A burst water-main, bubbling up through the surface of the road, curtain up at 9 p.m. on a summer's evening. I watched Act I for about an hour, with the water rising higher and higher, judged that by 10 p.m. no one was going to do anything about it and went to bed.

Next morning, the leak was almost a fountain, presaging exciting events, and then the telephone rang. The authorities requiring my assistance? But no, a booming voice, only too well known.

'Superior sport and games in the offing,' it cried. 'Drop every single thing and get over here without a single second's delay!'

I could just see the fountain, by leaning to the left, but still no sign of activity around the disaster area.

'The Prince,' the telephone boomed, '*and* the Princess Galli-Curci von und zu Schlumperhausen—' (it sounded something like that) – 'they're giving this enormous lunch party and she's simply mad to meet you. She's read all your—' (he sought to find a suitable appellation for my efforts in the literary field) – 'stuff,' he said. 'She's fearfully sorry about the short notice but she didn't know I knew you and she – Nina – looks almost exactly like Lollobrigida but with *class*—'

At that very moment the curtain rose on Act II of the water-main drama with the entry of none other than Jean, alert and efficient with a cigarette stub in the corner of his mouth, riding high in the cab of his motorized municipal tricycle, approaching the scene down the hill.

'I'm very sorry,' I told the telephone, 'but I cannot accept any social engagements today—'

'But, my God, look here, the Prince is even better looking than Cary Grant used to be and he's got this absolutely fabulous wine cellar—'

Jean deftly evaded the fountain in his motorized municipal trike and puttered on down the hill out of sight.

'I'm sorry,' I said, 'but we've got a burst water-main immediately outside the kitchen window and the water bailiff has just driven past it on his tricycle—'

'Water bailiff? On his tricycle?' He seemed to be repeating, phonetically, the sounds of some unfamiliar language. 'But, God, look—' The former urgency returned. I replaced the receiver and, on an afterthought, picked it up again and left it beside the apparatus, on the desk.

Jean came back again, up the hill, once more dodged the fountain and disappeared, but to be replaced, dead on cue, by Madame Carborundum and the lady whose car got assaulted in her own garage by the gravel lorry.

Both of them live at the bottom of the hill and, being below the leak, were obviously waterless. I joined them, around the fountain, and we had a good talk about the incompetence of the Mayor, Jean and the Department of Bridges and Roads. They, placed as they were, were loud in their affirmations that something should be done. I, with our water not too seriously affected, was more relaxed. I consoled them with the news that Jean had passed by on his tricycle and that something would surely happen soon.

I wanted to be there to see it, when it did, whatever form of carnival might be taking place at the Schlumperhausens, because I'd never seen men mending a burst water-main and absolutely had to be there to see how it was done.

I couldn't begin to guess how they would go about it and almost cheered when the builder – a sixteen-stone sphere, diameter 5 ft 3 ins, ears kept apart by a very small, flat beret – arrived in his van towing a huge, pale-blue compressor, accompanied by a nervous Algerian assistant.

It took them a lovely long time to unhook

the towing bar of the compressor. The spherical builder had the loudest voice east of Marseille, and used it at full power, until Abdallah got to work with the pneumatic drill, allowing the builder to lie down in the shade of the wall, and get some rest, after he'd turned off the water-main.

Only Abdallah's head was showing – 4.15 p.m. – when the phone rang again, some ass having replaced our receiver. 'Look,' it cried, 'you've simply got to get here – we're all in the pool and Nina's starkers—' I cut him off like lightning because our very own plumber had arrived with *his* van and a load of beautiful cast-iron collars, giant rubber washers and enormous nuts and bolts. I simply galloped down the road and watched, panting with excitement, while he cut the pipe with an extraordinary red instrument filled with razor-sharp wheels, removed about a yard of it and was replacing it with the iron collars when I saw the motor-cycle cop coasting down the road on his glittering, black machine.

Everything was being beautifully stage-managed, the copper an enormous asset in his white crash helmet, blue shirt, black boots and white pistol holster and even with a piece of paper clenched between his teeth – certainly a summons to be served on someone. And who should be behind him, like Sancho Panza to Don Quixote, but Jean on his municipal machine!

21

The copper got off his bike slowly, as they do, lifting a ponderous, splendidly menacing leg, and propped the bike on its stand. Jean parked beside him, but remained under his tricycle cowling.

Abdallah, down the hole, having restarted his pneumatic drill under our plumber's instructions, knew none of this and almost petulantly flicked his air-hose into a more convenient position. It knocked the police-man's motor-bike off its stand, throwing it with a bang against Jean's contrivance, in which he was still sitting.

I withdrew from the scene, being a mere supernumerary, to the orchestra stalls in our kitchen. I never like to be there when French policemen lose their temper, particularly those who ride motor-bicycles.

Through this brief interval I lost my grip on the plot. It clattered on, however, for another twenty minutes, with the copper and the round builder in full voice, accompanied by off-stage music from Abdallah's drill. Almost without warning, then, the final curtain swished down and everyone went away, leaving a muddy declivity in the ground.

I never found out what happened to the copper's piece of paper, but really the whole performance had been satisfactory in the extreme.

In comparison with all this grand opera Nina, starkers in the pool, would have had the draw of a dog-act in a fading music-hall bill.

Kinda dressy

All we pyjama men know, do we not, when our three – or at the very maximum four – pairs of night wear begin to 'go'.

We can diagnose the symptoms only too well. Trouser cords beginning to fray, or even worse, one end disappearing into the tunnel so that we have to knot the material in the front in a lump which, if lain upon during sleep suggests the intrusion of a croquet ball into the bed, probably by a rival or a mere practical joker.

We get elbow bursting, so that the forearm part of the sleeve is retained only by the inner seam. In fact, in terminal cases of pyjama 'going' it's really only the seams that hold the whole garment together, including one useful button down the front, all the others having been rent away by normal wear and tear.

For married men pyjamas, even in this decaying state, seem to have at least another six months' mileage in them until, that is, they are outlawed by wives on the grounds that the well-laundered but nonetheless just visible stains of coffee and egg on the front are putting them off their own bed-breakfast of weak-kneed China tea with a slice of lemon.

It was for all these reasons, presented with unarguable strength, that I decided to divert my three existing veterans to car polishing, shoe cleaning, etc., and to buy some more, once again to the number three – one on, one in the laundry and one just in case.

To this end I swung into a *distingué* gentlemen's emporium in London's West End and went straight up to an executive behind the very first counter, a young man with notably wide lapels on his jacket and a dangerous Mexican moustache. 'Would you be so kind,' I said, 'to direct me to the elephant's pyjama department?' Shopping for *anything* is such agony I always like to give it a bit of spin.

He came straight back. 'I regret, sir,' he said, 'but we no longer do them.'

Hurt, but recovering quickly, I reposted with, 'You mean to tell me that you no longer deal in large-size pyjamas despite a vast clientele of huge visiting Americans, enormous Germans and probably substantial Arabs, although admittedly it's difficult to tell how big they are beneath their robes?'

'We simply do not do them at all, sir.'

For a second I thought I might have dashed into a shop, by accident, catering for ladies and in a position, therefore, to take delivery of a flame-coloured sateen nightie large enough to cover fifteen stone, but then

24

the sight of an even bigger man trying to struggle into a leather coat that might have fitted a jockey confirmed that I was in men's wear.

'You mean to say that you don't sell pyjamas of any kind!'

'No, sir.' A very good, slight cough, out of deference for my years, then he let me have it. 'You see, sir, pyjamas are really no longer being worn. Quite out of fashion, in fact.'

'But that's mad. I grant you that pyjamas for certain nocturnal – ah – exercises might be as incommoding as Olympic high-jumping in plus-fours but what about a chilly night when the central heating's been cut off owing to industrial dispute and someone's punctured your hotty-botty?'

'You could add another blanket, sir.'

'Against the skin?'

He felt a change of subject was due. 'I believe you'll be back in London next month, sir,' he said, adding an almost kind smile. 'I promise you, on your return, by hook or by crook, I shall have a pair of pyjamas for you.'

'What has the world come to if you can only get a pair – *one* pair – of pyjamas by hook or by crook?'

'It's the modern mode, you see, sir,' he said, slamming a door on the whole matter.

I bet you that some public relations genius has been messing around with this shop's image, on the grounds that if the punk rockers can make a fortune out of nauseating

25

the world surely a *distingué* gentlemen's haber-dashery can shoot right to the top of the pops by selling their clients the idea that if you don't wear pyjamas in bed you're out of sight, you're where it's at, you're *in*, thereby sinking the trade of hundreds of rival establishments who are still going to the trouble of stocking and selling pyjamas by the ton.

It's irritating enough to find fashion sticking its oar into the bedroom but even worse to find the fickle idiot shying away from the well-known fact that nearly all babies are bigger now than they used to be so that unless they begin smoking at four some of them are liable to turn into not necessarily fatter but certainly longer men.

I must admit it's some years since I've been a bigger baby – perhaps a kind of one-off job well before its time – but nonetheless I've still got a special case to plead before haber-dashers, except in America, all over the world.

For some reason, probably commercial, clothes seem to be made in miniscule quantities for men who are over six feet in height. Despite all this bigger baby stuff we seem to continue to be rarities or rare enough to be fobbed off with large cardigans, shirts and other gear so hideous in colour and design that they appear to be the result of a fault in the machinery rather than any rational plan.

(While I'm at it I'd like to take back my exception of America, where clothes for mini-giants guarantee their visibility at the range of three miles.)

Come shopping with me and see what happens.

I pick on almost any gentlemen's haberdasher, except those with lace shirts in the window, and I breeze in, a gallant old clipper with my top-gallants full of wind, and before they can say anything, or make the slightest move in my direction, I say – without punctuation or change in the level of the voice, 'Good morning I know you haven't any navy-blue jerseys with round or V-neck size 48 thank you goodbye.'

I come about, all-standing, and sail out again, leaving a vacuum in my wake.

This close-hauled work is the product of years of experience. If you let them play it their way you're going to be in there all during lunch, and probably miss the mid-afternoon apéritif break as well.

Their way is to say, 'Good morning, sir, are you socks, shirts, underwear, knitwear, jodhpurs—?' and so on, ranging over their whole stock-in-trade.

Then you put in your order. 'One navy-blue jersey with round or V-neck, size 48.' Then they put in their spanner. 'I don't theenk we can do the 48, sir. But I shall certainly have a look for you.'

For a long time they flick through a load of *turtle-necked* jerseys in canary yellow, cardinal red, sage and puce. I can see the sizes on the labels. They range from 38 to 42, and might accommodate one of my arms. Then they say, 'Were you looking for any particular colour, sir?' I put in my navy-blue bid for the second time, stressing once again the round or V-neck, and after a lot more scratching they come up with the correct article. They spread it out on the counter and look at it lovingly. 'There you are, sir,' they say, 'size 46.'

'I rather wanted size 48.'

'I'm afraid we don't do 48's, sir. Would you like to try on the 46?'

Off, then, in the bad old, hopeful days, with the mackintosh and the jacket and on with the 46 and it's obviously a size too small so off with it again and the hair style all rumpled and on with the jacket and the mackintosh and polite goodbyes and I feel like kicking in their window on the way out.

That's why I now say, 'Good morning I know you haven't any navy-blue jerseys with round or V-necks size 48 thank you good-bye,' and walk straight out, because *some* day one of them is going to say, 'By sheer chance, sir, we do have the article you have specified in size 48,' but it's going to be in the stock-room so they can't get at it immediately and in any case they've got another customer on their hands. A customer made to measure, by his wife.

I remember walking into a gentlemen's haberdasher so select that it was furnished with two sofas and only one assistant, and he was up to his neck in two Americans, and the two Americans were up to *their* necks in V-necked jerseys of every conceivable colour, size 40. It looked as if they'd been there for a long, long time, and into – at the moment – a black cashmere number.

'I don't think, sir,' the assistant was saying, both his voice and his mind badly frayed, 'I don't think you'll find that too dressy.'

'Well,' the American customer said, 'I think it's kinda dressy.' He turned to his wife. 'Honey,' he said, 'do you think that's kinda too – dressy?'

She looked at the garment for several minutes. 'I just want you to be comfortable in it, honey,' she said. 'I don't see you buying a sweater you're not gonna be comfortable in. Of course, it is kinda dressy.'

'I think it's kinda dressy,' her husband said, and then all three of them looked at the black cashmere sweater for a couple of hours.

At the end of this time the wife said, 'Maybe if you keep the dressy one and take the red sorta sporty one too?'

His brow furrowed. 'Which red sorta sporty one was that, honey?' he said. 'I didn't see any sorta red sporty one.'

I eased my position on the opposing sofa. The assistant – he was visibly shaking – produced a red item from the pile.

'Wow,' said the lady, 'now there's a sharp sweater.'

The husband looked at it for a few days. 'Yep,' he said, in the end, 'that surely is one sharp sweater. Honey,' he said, 'you don't think it's kinda—'

She divined his thoughts in a flash. 'Too sharp, you mean, honey?'

'Yep.'

'Well, I don't know. I guess it's kinda—'

I left. The maddening thing is that I *know* that shop has a navy-blue jersey size 48. But I also know I'll have to wait to get at it until those Americans go home to vote in their next Presidential election.

See you for five nails

With the total unexpectedness of a large bomb going off in a small tobacconist's at the back of Paddington station a crack of deafening thunder flattened the garden, followed by an endless glare of green light that could only have come from the other side of the moon.

Madame was the first to respond. She sprang straight up from her long chair beside the pool and sped for the house so quickly that for a moment I thought the lightning had touched her up, until I saw that she was only getting in out of the rain, which now began as though discharged from upon high by fire hoses.

In our rush to evade it George and Liz and I got jammed in the door of the pavilion. It was only our superior masculine strength that squeezed her out, otherwise we chaps would have got even wetter. Still, I was fairly comfortable after I'd added a large Greek rug to my bathing trunks.

We stood there looking out at Niagara from the inside – Niagara illuminated by livid green lightning that simply stood for long periods, without a flicker, in the night-black sky. We were marooned in the pavilion almost certainly for the rest of the afternoon, so that it was good news when George said that he happened to have a pack of cards in his bag and a little poker might help to pass the time.

Dressed in my Greek rug and bathing trunks, I had to allow to a certain shortage of specie whilst they, with their luggage to hand, must have some supply of pounds, travellers' cheques and whatever continental currencies they might have picked up on their recent travels. George – you could see he was nearly dealing them already – pointed out that with a box of matches we would have an ample reserve of counters that should see us through all but the most frenetic bout of gambling.

I found a box containing twenty-two matches. We took seven each. 'French franc per match,' I suggested, 'call it two old shillings.'

It seemed a bit sparse in the way of financial backing. I saw the plastic box of assorted toffees that some demented visitor had left behind. There were fifteen each. 'One toff two French francs,' I said, 'or four old bob.'

We began with a jackpot, which Liz opened first crack out of the box with two toffs and a match. 'Or,' she said, 'twenty-five pee,' introducing a new element. George won the hand, having drawn two to fill the middle of a revolting straight. I'd been in there punching with the hand I've held for the whole of my poker playing life – i.e. a pair of threes and a pair of fives – and had to hand over ten toffs and five matches. A couple of minutes later I was cleaned out owing Liz four toffs and six matches.

'If', I said, 'either or both of you would care to advance me, on note of hand alone, some old shillings, revalued guilder or even piastres, we could get on with the game.'

George considered it. 'I don't think we want to introduce *money* into it,' Liza said. 'At least, not yet.'

'Right,' I said. 'I'll be back.' With the Greek rug over my head I shot round the corner to the potting shed and came back with twenty-four nails, ten hooks covered with white plastic and a small screwdriver. 'One nail five old shillings,' I said, 'or two francs fifty centimes. One plastic hook ten francs or a pound sterling. The screwdriver stands in at a fiver.' We'd already come some way since the kindergarten days of the toffs and the matches.

'Just a moment,' Liz said, 'I'd like to make a list of the new currency.' She did so, with precision. 'One cannot be too careful,' she pointed out, 'with the floating stuff.'

The game went quite smoothly after that, with the ante at one nail, double with one white plastic hook, while you might get seen by twelve toffs and a couple of matches. Unfortunately, I was still getting my old blockbusting pairs of threes and fives, so that at one moment I had to nip round to the bank in the potting shed for eight brass screws at twenty francs each, in order to support a sudden run on my reserves.

I don't know what time it was when Madame appeared at the door of the pavilion. It was dark, but at least the rain seemed to have stopped. She looked at the table covered with cards, toffees, hooks, matches and all the rest of the international currency. 'Settle up,' she said. 'Dinner's ready.'

I don't like to think about the final account. Suffice it to say that if the fiduciary issue had not been turned into cash Liz would have had a dear little screwdriver, and George could have built a house with his nails and hooks and eaten toffee in it for ever.

All the gen on GBS

When I saw that Michael Holroyd had been appointed by the Shaw estate as biographer of George Bernard Shaw and would like to hear from anyone who had letters or information that might be of use to him I was out in a flash with the embossed notepaper and just about to indite him a line or two when I suddenly thought, 'Ayup, lad – sithee, there's owt for nowt.'

I was probably thinking about D. H. Lawrence at the time. I used to know him well, too. I stole his hat when I was four. Larry – as we used to call him – had been booming away at my mother for hours about feminine sexuality and I got sick of it so I put his hat or, rather an unpleasant cloth cap, behind the sofa, reporting to my mother in an undertone, 'I hided his hat.'

My mother thought it amusing and relayed the story to Lady Ottoline Morell, who made no response, being busy at the time with Bertrand Russell.

Here – I'm *giving* the stuff away with both hands, pages of biographical material for nothing. Let's narrow it down to Shaw or

'Bernie', as I called him at the time.

I was ten when I met him in the Great Southern Hotel, Parknasilla, Co Kerry, where he was writing *St Joan*. My parents, of course, used to keep open house in London for him and Lawrence and Lady Ottoline, naturally enough the latter with Bertie Russell in tow – is there *no* method of getting rid of those two?'

Well, anyway, Bernie was writing *St Joan* but before beginning work in the morning he used to go down to the little harbour to have a swim, wearing a long-legged, blue and white striped bathing suit with sleeves down to the elbows. My sister and I used to watch him with no little amusement, as the long, narrow, reddish head sank and resurfaced time after time. He was probably clearing his brains, having got to the difficult bit about the Dauphin. Well, anyway – ('well, anyway' seems to be built into the biographical narrative style) – well, anyway, after Bernie had had one of his morning mind-clearings and gone back to the hotel we found my father and mother and cried out to them in unison, 'We seen a silly old seal in a stripey suit,' and at that moment Bernie stepped out from behind a screen wearing his dressing-gown and the aforesaid piece of apparel and he did not even smile.

One day my father took all six of us in his open four-seater for a drive through the Gap of Dunloe, Biddy and I probably sitting on my mother's knee in front, so as not to annoy the Shaws. I got the impression that Mrs Shaw – Charlotte – was not too fond of children, because when, later on, my mother took a photograph of the outing the Shaws are seen to be sitting at the very end of a low wall and my father and we kids at the other.

Well, anyway, after I turned journalist and came to London, looking for more money than the *Irish Times* could provide, I dropped a cheery line to Bernie saying that while I quite understood he didn't know anything about journalism he might know of some other openings in the literary field over which I might cast an eye. By that time he was probably up to the hubcaps in *Back to Methuselah*. Anyway, he didn't reply.

The years unfolded and the Sage was about to celebrate his ninety-second, third or fourth birthday at Ayot St Lawrence. I went down to interview him and found the whole village jammed not only with other journalists but also with news film crews, and no one could get near him. They had tried everything, but his housekeeper – (*Library please check name*) – his housekeeper refused even to answer the doorbell. One reporter, somewhat red-faced and wearing a brown suit, showed me an X-ray picture with, written across the top of it, 'Dear Mr Shaw – I've had one break, please give me another.' He was indignant. 'I shoved it under the door,' he said, 'and she shoved it straight back again.' He looked at

36

his message with obviously hurt pride. 'I borrowed it from my brother,' he said. 'It's his knee.'

Well, anyway, I wrote Shaw a note – I always seemed to be writing to him in those days – reminding him of Parknasilla and craving the favour of a brief interview. I pushed it under the door and it came straight back again unopened. As I left the village I found a newsreel man with shears cutting a hole in Shaw's hedge. 'This is where we got the ole geezer from last year,' he said. I peered through the hole. The famous summer-house was clearly visible, but appeared to be unoccupied, so I went home.

Well, Mr Holroyd – Michael, Mike – there's the whole dossier on GBS. Full acknowledgement, old lad, and see my agent about the money.

Only the players are vile

In my present bookworm-ridden monastic – without even the Benedictine – life I'd been ploughing gently page by page through this (advt) 'explosive, brutal, bloodthirsty intrigue' that had been troubling, in a notably dis-ordered way, every single thing that had so far happened to an emergent African nation, putting up at the same time my own bitter battle against dropping off to sleep when, without so much as the snapping of a twig in the jungle, someone slipped an assegai up to the maker's name right through my ribs.

I mean, I got a terrible shock on Page 336. There I was, dozing gently downhill towards the eagerly awaited end, when these words, written in still smoking blood, sprang at me from their otherwise innocuous surroundings. Let me write them down as best I can. Here goes:

'The British High Commissioner played a rotten game of golf. But his early years in the Foreign Service had been mostly in Ireland, which explained his poor game because any golfer worth his handicap knew that the "great" Irish golf courses were a tourist agency myth.'

Can you imagine a – a thing like that being said when the worst crimes we've had to put up with so far have been routine rape, murder, arson, treachery, suspected canna- balism and white politicians telling lies? Of all the gratuitous, toffee-nosed, smugly arro- gant, stone-ignorant accusations. As well charge the caddy master at, say, Portmarnock with collecting all the flag-sticks and setting them on fire under the secretary's wife in the pot bunker on the right of the eighteenth green, incinerating her like Joan of Arc. A possibility, may I suggest, as far removed as any British High Commissioner catching a rotten game of golf by playing in Ireland, on 'great' courses which are purely a tourist agency myth.

It's a well-known fact, to anyone who knows anything not only about golf in Ireland, but about anything at all, that all Irish golf-courses are round about as unplayable as Mount Everest, not because of their precipitous nature but because of the psychological factors involved – factors provided *in toto* by the local players.

How well I remember the British Amateur played at Portmarnock in 1949, and some of the exciting events that preceded it. On the Sunday before it began the late Henry Longhurst denounced the choice of Portmarnock for this event, on the grounds that before he could watch it unfolding he had to present his British passport to Southern Irish immigration authorities – a ludicrous (to his keen mind) anomaly that drove him cold with rage for several lines.

It was to counter this anti-Irish golf propaganda – at least as far as the British Amateur Championship was concerned – the late Robert Maire Smyllie, editor of the *Irish Times*, urged me to accompany him on a trial round. He was a big man – sixteen-stone – of immense dignity, who wore a five-gallon dark green sombrero and a long, curving pipe, even while playing tennis – his rather better game – so that on the first tee his caddy, a male child of about eleven years of age, didn't have the courage to refuse him the use of a niblick, rather than a driver, for his opening blow.

It was a stroke, into the teeth of a chilly east wind, that left a scar several feet long on the turf, whilst the ball, at an angle of 90°, finished on the pebbly beach. 'On safari, Dr Livingston,' Mr Smyllie said to his caddy, and set off seawards without further remark.

By a series of what many people thought to be fortunate accidents I got through the first three rounds of the Championship itself, and in the fourth reached the eighteenth all-square with Billy O'Sullivan, a formidable hero, but in a deep gravel pit one hundred yards left of the green. I slashed at it savagely, hoping to bound back off the invisible clubhouse, or Billy's head, only to leave it beside the hole, to win an exciting match.

And was it not at a West of Ireland Championship in Ballybunion, speeding around town in a little red sports car, that I was warned by a huge policeman, 'You're puttin' the heart across the civilian population in that little red yoke.' Beaten, of course, in the first round, by a local civilian, feeling myself to be as popular as an armed and uniformed invader.

Playing a rotten game, just like any British High Commissioner, but through no fault, self-evidently, of the course.

No time to dream

The trouble about us hard-bitten – well, half-chewed – old sea dogs is that after many years on the bounding main we tend to wake with an audible click after the lightening passage of only four hours a-poundin' the ear'ole in the 'ammock, not that that Devonian *patois* – if Devonian it be – becomes a retired Chief Petty Officer in the Irish Marine Service, not that now we're 'notting', as it were, I'm going to be towed away by that theme, unlesss by specific request, accompanied by a suitable emolument.

Anyway, taking two quick round turns on the narrative before it runs away with me, I get four hours sleep per night irrespective of the time at which I slip off me bell-bottoms and slide into the basket. Amazing, really. And, by the look of it, a wholly unnecessary miracle to ninety-eight per cent of the rest of the world. When they get into it they like to remain there, unconscious, until beaten out of it with sticks, fire, explosions or the need to go to some place of work.

These four hours of mine, stingy as they may seem to the dedicated ear-pounders, are in themselves round, complete and perfect, almost machine-made, one might say.

Give me a bed, a pair of glasses, Tolstoi or a paperbacked book with some gravy on the outside and on the inside irreparable sludge, and within five or six pages I'm doing the best and soundest sleeping the world has ever seen, unmarred by twitching, shouting, blanket tugging and the other excesses perpetrated by people who regard sleeping not as an art but as a hog-like self-indulgence, in which they will go on indulging themselves until someone whips them out of the pit by the back leg.

It's the irrespective bit about this art that creates trouble for so many people and in particular – absolutely mountains of it – for myself. If I am going to wake up from this perfect sleeping irrespective of the time at which I have set it in motion I can find myself wide awake and in spanking form at 11.45 at night.

It might seem strange to some that a fully-grown man should find 7.30 p.m. a rational time to go to bed, provided that he finds himself in even the rudiments of good health. On the other hand we perfect, short sleepers – we must be as rare as hairy, spotted elephants – are utterly helpless to deny the call when it comes, at a time when other people are still wondering what they would like for dinner. Upstairs at 7.30 p.m., glasses, Tolstoi, drivel and – bang! – we're gone at

7.45, to wake up in top form for a new day at fifteen minutes before midnight.

I have thought a lot, having had plenty of time for it, about what to do *re* this situation, seeing that other people in the house have not as yet gone to bed or are in it, already digging themselves into the oblivion that will endure for at least another eight to nine hours, unless violently disturbed.

The sensible thing for me to do, having woken at 11.45 p.m. after a good night's sleep, is to get up, cook myself a substantial breakfast and hurl myself, much refreshed, into the activities of the day, whatever they may be at midnight.

But here, of course, I am beset with problems and difficulties. It is impossible to fry a quiet breakfast. Bacon sizzling at midnight brings people, who have been previously asleep, skidding wildly down the stairs, throwing water in all directions, calling for police, the fire brigade, tearing down the curtains before they go up in flames, to be poleaxed to a halt only in the doorway of the kitchen upon seeing a man, fully dressed, slipping a couple of tomatoes and a slice of bread into a smoking frying-pan, like as not with a shy smile.

But say, now, one settles for silent scrambled eggs with very soft toast and all that goes down without breaking the plate, coughing over coffee or further alarms and then— But what, at midnight?

Gardening with a torch? Writing letters on velvet with a felt pen? Going for a walk and getting hurled by the police into the paddy wagon for loitering after dark with intent to do something nasty? Better, perhaps, just to sit in a chair, thinking until lunch, which surely could be taken as late at 8 a.m. Followed, naturally, by dinner at mid-day and an early bed by 2 p.m. To be up again for breakfast at 6.30, admittedly at a time when others are having their pre-dinner drinks, leaving them still rioting around at 10.30 p.m. when I'm trying to take a bite of lunch.

The thing that really interests me about this is how long it would take me to carry on with this sequence until I woke up at 9 a.m., in synchronization with the rest of the world. Unfortunately, it is now exactly 11.30 a.m. and therefore bedtime, so I'll have to leave all that for another day – or night.

Breaking – not entering

It's so irritating at times not to be a competent burglar.

I do not have reference, of course, to these untutored breaking and entering lads who turn their hand to other people's property because they've got nothing else to do, being on strike at the time and tiring of getting attacked, hour after hour, by militant police when all they are doing is leaning against a wall, holding a literate explanation, on cardboard, of why they are totally peaceably picketing.

Thanks to television these lads don't even have to break before they enter. All they have to do is to find a shingled Tudor residential area, preferably with two cars in the drive, and nip around the back to find the ladder that gives access to the open bedroom window, the frame of which was being painted, very badly, by Derek during the course of the afternoon until he got sick of it. Derek and Caroline are now, at 9.30 p.m., looking at television, all their senses sufficiently numbed to allow the burglars in the bedroom to demolish Caroline's dressing-table with an axe, in search of her goodies, without interference by interested parties.

Perfectly straightforward work of this kind doesn't interest me. The skills that I seek are those of the bent wire and celluloid strip merchants who insert the home-made tools of their trade into the selected lock, give it a bit of a twist and they're in. And never more so than on last Tuesday morning at 8.25 a.m. when I found that the master hairdresser who trims our olive trees had gone, inexplicably leaving a waterproof anorak behind him, on a bush, as evidence that he had been here, and left.

It took me some time to find out why. The reason was that all his instruments were in my potting shed, clearly visible through the window, but irremediably out-of-bounds seeing that the door was locked and the key, which I store in the cleft of a tree beside the shed, had been dislodged during the night by some unknown influence and must now be lying in or under the mass of cut branches which the master hairdresser very sensibly leaves for me to clear up.

What a disaster. What shame. What a disgrace. And even more disgraceful when Jean came back with some more tools, to find me rooting like a pig on a truffle run in the mountain of silvery green debris into which the key had plunged. He was most polite. He begged me not to derange myself. He said it wasn't grave. All would go well. He went up the ladder and the rain, a perfectly normal element in sunny Provence, came belting down all over again so he went home for good, getting the benefit of his waterproof anorak.

I stood for some time under a very old golf umbrella, glaring at the maddening keyhole in the potting shed door. I know what the key looks like. It's simply a small bar with what looks like a perfectly regular rectangle sticking out of one end. There must be millions of them in the world, all exactly the same. We even have thousands here, for indoor doors, french windows, window windows but not a single one of them will open the potting shed door. How can a tiny rectangular flat knob be so different to all other flat knobs everywhere? And, above all else, how can a competent burglar replace them with a piece of bent wire, or a strip of celluloid? Bent wire and, particularly, celluloid, don't look like a key in any of its three simple dimensions. How *do* the burglars do it?

I assaulted the keyhole with all four of the screwdrivers that have failed to open the door on the many occasions when the key has disappeared, with the usual negative result. I bent a piece of wire and shoved it in and screwed it around and nothing happened. I thought of a credit card, it being the only bit of celluloid I knew, and could see clearly the subsequent correspondence: 'Dear Sirs, my credit card is stuck in the door of the potting shed so please forward another one by return of post—'

I began to sift the branches with the left hand, holding the very old golf umbrella in the right. A stack of foliage at least thirty cubic feet in size. As a very young golfer I have actually prayed to St Anthony, on my knees, in dense gorse, begging for the return of my Goblin. I did so now, in the same position, but obviously putting St Anthony off *his* stroke by sulphurous thoughts about

47

breaking the window, smashing down the door, blowing it up, selling the house, emigrating to New Zealand – anything to solve the problem of this obscenely locked and unopenable door.

It was raining more heavily than ever when I found the key, a miserably little rusty object hiding under the crushed leaf of a geranium, buried in its turn by fifty tons of branches. I opened the door of the potting shed, left it open and put the key, for safety, in a new secret place.

I have been looking for it ever since. But, at least, the door is open.

No jug of wine –
no loaf of bread

All thinking persons, such as ourselves, tend to regard the fanatic hobbies of others with a cool indifference.

In the case of the more disgusting hobbies – the collection of Toby Jugs, water-colours of Lake Windermere – this indifference can mount on a rough day to open derision.

Take the case of a coarse fisherman. Imagine a man in a woollen hat sitting under a coloured umbrella in drenching rain on a small canvas stool beside some reeking river behind the gas-works, rolling pellets of whole-meal bread and marmalade, with a squirt of soya sauce, the better to entrap a perch or a dace so miniature in size as to be verging on the invisible, in the certain knowledge that when, if ever, he lands one it will not be only invisible but inedible, and most probably dead.

To all us thinking persons it would seem impossible to picture an activity more cheer-less, or more futile – apart from the howling boredom of going on a diet.

Millions of people, every day, go on diets and stay on diets and come off diets and then begin another diet, and listening to them talking about it is worse than having to wrench an ear around the coarse fisherman's detailed explanation of why he adds soya sauce to his wholemeal bread and marmalade.

There is a religious ferocity about the dieters. If one says, being polite, 'But surely half a shredded carrot in your salad wouldn't do any harm—' their eyes roll, their whole body trembles, as they denounce the deadly carrot and all its works.

With plastic pocket gauges they count calories or carbohydrates, or they eat only bananas with buttermilk, so that the whole simple matter of filling the tum-tum until it doesn't want any more becomes a scientific experiment checked by invisible overseers in white coats, tolerance 2-thou. of an inch, and if you get it wrong you die.

I'm on one of those diets now.

This is the first diet I've been on.

That's not entirely true. When I was working for the *Irish Times* in Dublin I gave up smoking and drinking on the morning of 19 December, 1938. A public relations man came into my office with a Christmas present of a box of (small) cigars, and a bottle of whiskey. He said he hoped I would enjoy them though he, himself, had given up smoking and drinking for ever. We looked at the gifts and we both began – 11.15 a.m. – smoking and drinking again.

Apart from that shortish spell I've never been on a diet before, but I'm now on a diet that produces the feeling of being locked in an iron lung, with the machinery turned off.

I got into the lung through Madame reading a book by somebody called Dr Robert Atkins who promised us that if we followed his diet we would not only become ten pounds thinner for life but that that life, thanks to the normalization of our metabolic systems, would be one of garlanded, health-ridden teenagers in Arcady.

This second section – though not in the Doctor's precise words – was the one that got Madame, whose weight hasn't changed by more than a couple of pounds in years.

So, last Monday, we began by giving up bread, alcohol, root vegetables, potatoes, milk, sugar, fruit, spaghetti, macaroni and chewing gum, the latter being the easiest seeing that chewing gum has never befouled this house, nor ever will.

It was Items One and Two that switched off my pumping machinery. I couldn't see, I said, how anyone could choke down an egg, a kipper, grilled bacon and mushrooms, frankfurter sausages or any other breakfast medicament without some kind of bread to suck up the life-giving juices involved. Furthermore, after years of living in France, I can't face even a cheese biscuit without a bottle of wine to see it on its way. I said that, too. 'And,' I said, 'when the vesper hour arrives the absence of a drop of John Barleycorn can only bring on paralysis, madness and death.'

Last Monday I had, for breakfast, two boiled eggs – consumption time fifteen seconds per egg and that was it. Lunch was a steak, a green salad and two bottles of mineral water. For vespers I had another kind of mineral water and a third kind of dinner, with roast chicken and some more lettuce. I had a night-cap of mineral water and some more at 6 a.m., with ice to jazz it up.

By yesterday morning I had lost Dr Atkins required ten pounds, in something – it seemed to me – of a hurry, in that the garlanded, golden life of Arcady obviously hasn't had time to catch up.

Moroseness appears to be my prevailing mood, but at least I don't talk about my diet.

The fact is that I don't have the strength to speak while my companions slosh the stuff down by the bucketful, condemning themselves to a fat, corrupt and happy old age.

All night in front of a pint!

I was on my daily battle course through the back pages of *Nice Matin*, wriggling under the profuse wire of local football – tons of it with banner headlines – dozens of minor but intimidating obstacles like handball, basketball, cycling, *boules*, Scrabble, hockey on the lawn, tennis of the table and the usual pictures of Omar Sharif playing bridge in urgent need of a hair-cut, when I suddenly burst out into open country, on to the green desert of Connemara.

I can tell yah, lads, it fair put the heart acrost me. There was dear ole Connemara, competin' in competition wit the thremendous news that Nice had bet the boots offa Beziers two goals to wan and it takin' up nearly halfa the page of the paper, under the headline, as long as your arm, *DANS LE DESERT VERT DU CONNEMARA*.

I trew meself on this piece like a starvin' lion after a juicy young goat and got the shock of me life at the very first sentence.

'Curious,' it said, 'these Irish who, turning the back on the television, get together in a bar every evening to sing all night long in front of a pint of Guinness.'

I must relapse into vulgar English to make adequate comment upon this astonishing assertion. Admittedly, it is eight years since I've been in Connemara, but nonetheless I'm prepared to bet that while British television is readily available free of charge on the east coast of Ireland it would want a lot more push to get as far as the west, leaving the natives of that area confined to Irish television, in front of which you could hang around for the rest of your life without getting a flash of your topless. The meanest public-house, as far as ten miles away, is therefore preferable to an evening with Téléfish, leaking out from Dublin.

But singing all night long, in front of *a* pint of Guinness, is inconceivable on two important counts. Firstly, *three* pints are needed to lubricate the vocal cords and at least *two* more must be taken to entangle them in song, rather than the verbal destruction of everyone for miles around, including one's own wife, the parish priest, the local solicitor and that big lump of a sergeant from the barracks, the reference being, of course, to the police station.

Secondly, this aforesaid 'big lump' constitutes an exceedingly dangerous threat to 'all night' singing. He's liable to be in there like avenging fury six minutes after closing time, particularly if he knows there's someone in there he's got it in for, possibly the local bookmaker, with his head laid back, stuck into the tenor part of *Some Enchanted Evening* with a pint in his hand and several more lined up in front of him on the bar. Practically jail bait, for the outraged law. In any case, early end of choral evening, until the following night, when the same thing happens again.

Feeling I'd dealt, comprehensively, with this first line of the piece about Connemara, I had a look at the next one, only to find yet another pardonable misinterpretation. It said, 'Joyous or grave, the atmosphere gives the impression of great fraternity from which the traveller is not excluded, on the contrary.'

On the other contrary, the most revolting looking traveller, smelling like a polecat, with crossed eyes and only one tooth in the front of his head, would have to fight like a tiger to *get* himself excluded from the great fraternity, every single member of which is fighting to wrap the stranger in his arms, not from fraternal love but simply because this fella, wherever he comes from, has never been seen around these parts before and has therefore never had the benefit of the conversation, including a song or two, a couple of card tricks and the fruity local gossip provided by the fraternity's every member. But, if you don't mind, one at a time, and I'm first. This hapless stranger is a new audience for a well-tried act, an act so well-tried, in fact, that people as far away as Limerick Junction know every word and gesture of it inside out, and tend to leave with the speed of lightning the moment the curtain goes up. The fact that this fella is French and by the look on his face understands about one word in every hundred doesn't matter. With a good grip on the sleeve of his jacket you can be sure he'll still be there when you get to the distant end of the story about what you said to poor Willie Yeats in 1923, including the reprise of what he said and the good one that Jimmy Joyce came in with at the heel of the hunt.

Towards the end of this interesting article I learnt the surprising news that no fewer than 51,000 French people settled in Southern Ireland last year, up from only 22,000 in 1968.

Imagine 51,000 Frenchies who haven't heard a word from me, personally, about the Irish Marine Service and De Valera's first plan to put us into green bell-bottomed trousers – and that's only just for starters. Just a bunch of sitting ducks.

It's a pity they're so far away.

Gurf with hernia

Ploog, the Plasticine – the Polythene – the Pleiostine – anyway, Ploog, the first pre-historic man to invent drains must have lived on top of a hill. He invented drains by pulling the plug out of his bath and then immediately looking out of the window to see how his wife was getting on with chopping up his breakfast dinosaur. To his fury he saw that his bath water was pouring down all over his wife, not that that was what enraged Ploog. What got his goat – an animal of which he had never heard, seeing that it hadn't been invented – what got Ploog's goat was the fact that his bath was washing all over his breakfst. So he gave his wife a shovel and told her to dig a drain – the word came to him in a flash – to divert the water from the dinosaur chopping up area.

That's not true. The *very first* man to invent drains was Gurf, who lived below Ploog at the bottom of the hill, in a deep valley. Finding Ploog's bath water endlessly pouring into his study he attacked Ploog with a club. Ploog won that one so that after Gurf had recovered he dug a drain – he'd learnt the word from Ploog – all round his house and then dug a deep hole on the other side which, without any help at all from Ploog, he called a soak-away.

That's how drains came to be invented, and since that ever so distant day no one has ever been able to think of a method of making them work any better, despite some of the most gallant improvisations ever seen on the face of the earth.

Of course, I don't really believe in Ploog or Gurf either, but when one finds the same drain blocked for the seventh time in the same place it makes it a little easier if one can shovel the blame on to someone else.

It's the awful similarity of the thing that kills. First of all the water takes for ever to run out of the sink and then it starts to gobble as it runs out of the bath and then I take up the four small manhole covers in front of the house and all of them are filled to the brim with a grey, greasy liquid decorated with yellow blobs. After that I make the slow, sad pilgrimage down to the garage and come back with the length of stiff, yellow hosepipe still caked with the grey grease from the last de-blocking and begin pushing it into each manhole in turn until it will go no further. At the end of the day's work the level of the grey, greasy liquid remains unchanged, so Madame rings up the plumber and he never arrives. By the following week most of the grey, greasy liquid has seeped

57

away so that we can begin having two-inch baths again until the tide comes – and stays – in once more.

The trouble is that our soak-away, unlike Gurf's, is *above* the level of the house, thanks to the planning of an English architect (?) working, uneasily, in France. We endured this for years and then had it dug down to the depth of ten feet through – as it turned out – solid rock. A citizen from Algiers was down there, with a pneumatic drill, for three weeks, and used to walk into trees on his way home. However, before the bath water could cascade into this immense pit it had to make its way slightly up hill, leaving all kinds of deposits behind which I have to shove along with the stiff, yellow hosepipe once every couple of months. Except that last week it wouldn't budge, provoking the most severe crisis imaginable because we've just had all the paving stones in the small garden torn up and a cement base laid for the future laying of tiles and naturally enough the cement base won't dry while the drains are blocked and the tile layers propose to leave us for ever in two days' time, whether the tiles are laid or not and they can't lay the tiles on wet cement. An absolutely prehistoric situation.

This was where I invented one of the most gallant improvisations ever seen on the face of the earth. I attached a chisel to the end of the hosepipe with a metal clip and shoved it up the drain. Just like a knife through butter.

Until it stuck. I waggled it about a bit, but no further progress, so I dragged out the hose-pipe and found I'd left the chisel and the metal clip behind, about two-thirds of the way up the drain.

Now, I find I have – literally – ruptured myself, probably from laughing at the whole situation, and am taking the whole thing delicately back to London for gouging, shoving back and stitching up.

I shall be sorry not to be at home when the plumber if he ever comes, finds what's lying in wait for him up that drain.

Sildiers loo sart

It is to be regretted that that great news-paper, the *Duly Belegraph*, appears now to have come out on the other side of a par-ticularly rich Howling Madness phase and returned to the rigidities of the English language.

We of the fancy love the Howling Mad-nesses so well that we send them to one another all over the world, in case a moment of inattention might have led the other to overlook a particularly well-spotted specimen.

Only the other day, for instance, an

observer in Bangkok sent me, in a large envelope, a single line from the *Tennisgraph* that read, 'He threw his arms wife'. There was no covering note, because that's how we do it, not wishing to interfere with the private speculations of fellow members.

'He threw his arms wife.'

Perfect, giving the reader – instantly – the feeling that his brain has been given a half-turn so that the pointed ends are in line with his ears. 'He threw his arms wife' propels one straight into the fifth dimension where nothing seems to be exactly recognizable, or is it, and if it is what does it mean, if it means anything?

I came to the conclusion that 'He threw his arms wife' meant that this unknown individual had thrown his arms out wife-size – i.e. sufficiently far apart to encompass a wife if a wife had been standing in front of him – and sent one of my own straight back to Bangkok. Not a wife – it's that half-turn of the brain that does it – but a cutting of my own, which read, 'Mr Gavin Thurston, the Conores aid, "Two notes were found".'

'I'd been staring at it for hours. Who could this Conore be, to whom Mr Gavin Thurston was aid? I had never heard of anyone holding the legal post of Conore, but there was no doubt that Mr Gavin Thurston was in court at the time. And which of them announced the discovery of the two notes? For relief I turned to a large and simple slab of Howling

Madness, reading it aloud for several minutes in an authoritative voice. You might like to try it yourself.

'It is an amusing dramatization of what actually resemblance to the actual course happened but it bears no of events.'

I admit that the middle bit is not too easy – all this actually resemblance and actual course stuff – until you get into the swing of it, but there is no doubt whatever about the total finality of, 'It bears no of events'. If anyone were to tell me, seven times in a row, loudly, that 'It bears no of events', I would believe him implicitly, without having the remotest concept of what he was talking about. That is the essence of a good Howling Madness – the appearance of containing logic until you bear down upon it, when it splinters into a million pieces in your mind, bearing – as it obviously does, or does it? – no of events.

In the world of Howling Madness we get dear little towns, probably on the Adriatic, like Genevo. I can see the honest fisherfolk of Genevo at this very moment, a-mending of their nets on the quayside. The only thing, in fact, I don't know about them is whether they call themselves Genevones, or Genevores, but I'm certainly going to go there one day and ask, if I can find where Genevo is.

We also get the sudden intrusion of food and drink into situations where they have no real place.

'Another sharp cut in oil output,' the *Daily*

Teregaugh informs me, 'has been made by Saudi Arabia in a further effort to reduce the world wine surplus.' And, in another neighbouring column, it seems that, 'A few voice spectrographs were bought by police forces five or ten sago.'

While it is just possible that Saudi Arabia was supplying petrol for the fortification of port I cannot imagine what the coppers are doing with all this old sago. Perhaps a bit has been left out in the middle and it's a police-car call sign. 'Five or ten sago – over and out'. Or, more probably, it's the thing they say while they are testing a voice spectrograph because the special sound of 'Five or ten sago' leaves an absolutely indelible print. Perhaps if criminals say, 'Five or ten sago' into a spectrograph it shows where they have been last Thursday night. Perhaps, perhaps, perhaps. It's all such exhausting conjecture.

'Sildiers ran to the A.A. guns at Beirut Airport.' Are they very thin soldiers, or Lebanese Marines? 'The only concessio nasked for was 7½%.' How can one possibly nask for a concessio, even if it is only seven and a half per cent?

Ah, good – a break. Mail from London. A single cutting:

'It is certainly right to discourage those who loo over their shoulder.'

Thank God. We're on firm ground at last.

Bare boards are best

The carpet has arrived, almost seven months to the day it was purchased in London, with the promise that delivery would be made within three weeks.

It arrived in quite a large pantechnicon from its penultimate port of call, a town about half an hour away from here called Vallauris. It is impossible to imagine what it was doing there because all that goes on in Vallauris is the manufacture of souvenir pottery in shades of livid puce, ginger, deep purple and lime green.

The carpet, however, survived this experience and made it, at last, to our door. It looked like a long and enormous worm, wrapped in sacking, and it weighed sixty kilos – the poundage of a well developed woman. The driver of the van dragged it into the garage, pouched a bank-note with the speed of an adder, and drove away.

Late that afternoon, having wormed it up the narrow staircase with the right-angle turn, we spread it out under the furniture in the bedroom and then gave it a bit of a tug and then another tug and then dragged it around ferociously, upsetting several chairs and the desk until we reached the conclusion which had been on its way for some time, that the carpet was too wide for the room. On either side it was climbing up the wall.

Madame, very quiet, very steely, examined one of these mounting edges. 'That,' she said, 'is not the carpet I ordered seven months ago.'

I moved towards the door, in case she was going to tear it to pieces with her bare hands.

'On the carpet I ordered,' she continued in the same tone of voice, as tense as a bent saw, 'the two ends were taped but the sides weren't so I asked the young man in the carpet department to have it taped all round and he said he would see to it.' She wrenched up about a ton of carpet with one hand. 'None of this is taped,' she said. 'Not even the ends. After seven months.'

Like a machine-gunner getting in behind his weapon she settled herself at her desk, in the middle of the wrong carpet, and drew the typewriter towards her. 'First of all,' she said, almost conversationally, 'I'm going to tell them not to tell me it's my fault, and then go on from there.' The typewriter, red hot, began spitting out discarded shells.

When their reply came Madame read it twice, without speaking. She put it down. 'As I thought,' she said. 'Straight between the eyes. Straight back into my teeth.' She held up the letter by one corner. 'This executive here,' she said, 'believes that many of my problems with the carpet have been caused by genuine misunderstandings. That is, he is telling me I don't know how to buy a carpet, that I don't know anything about carpets and that none of this would have happened if I hadn't tried to buy a carpet from them. In the matter of taping,' she went on levelly, 'he says that the salesman concerned "has no recollection" and there is no record of receiving my instructions to tape. Furthermore, he informs me that they never tape this type of carpet because it doesn't need it and in any case I have not been charged for the taping that didn't happen. Urging me,' she pointed out, 'to look upon the bright side.'

Briefly, she reached out for someone's throat. 'You will remember,' she said, having relaxed again, 'how they screwed up the French Customs by ascribing the country of the carpet's origin to New Zealand, rather than to the United Kingdom? "Unfortunately", he said, "it happens to be true and therefore we could not avoid saying no". Wherein,' she asked me, 'lies that particular misfortune? What is unfortunate about a carpet that is made in New Zealand? I'll tell you. Me. If I hadn't bought that carpet they wouldn't have had to tell anyone it was made in New Zealand and everyone could have gone to bed early. It's my fault – again.'

Simultaneously, she snapped shut her eyes and her teeth, opened up, and proceeded.

'He says here he has to acknowledge a considerable delay in the dispatch. That's good, generous acknowledging of something we've known for seven months. But then he goes on to say that it was only partly their fault "in that there was some delay in their Packing Department", and the rest of the fault belongs to the transport company, "who informed us the goods would be delivered on 6 December". But we all know, don't we, whose fault it really was. Mine! For ordering the wrong carpet and wanting it taped when it didn't need it and cluttering up the Packing Department and causing the unfortunate transport company to have to tell lies about 6 December. Mine – all mine.'

She rose purposefully to her feet. 'I am now going,' she said, 'upstairs, to climb up the wall with the carpet.'

Mod cons

How to make a lump of loot in a hurry without too finicky a regard for the moral issues (if any) involved, was the subject of our discourse – a theme which, by its very popularity, tends to become wearisome these days.

We had ranged over all the old tried and tested methods – dropping the name of a Sheik or two, forming a private bank, slipping the proceeds into the Cayman Islands via the Seychelles – when Mrs Murple, not one of the swiftest financial negotiators of the age, suddenly said, 'Mrs Stifflewood very nearly had my lot.'

(In the interests of prudence I have changed the names of both ladies, in that Mrs Stifflewood might just conceivably have been on the level and if she was she'd have me by the back of the neck but, there, I'm running away with myself – and, boy would *that* be a love match!)

Anyway, Mrs Murple suddenly said that Mrs Stifflewood had very nearly had her (Mrs Murple's) lot. The ingenuity of it instantly aroused my commercial interest, which says a lot for Mrs Stifflewood's plan, seeing that my commercial interest scarcely ever gets out of bed.

Briefly, Mrs Murple wanted to spend a month in London and, therefore, put an advertisement in an English newspaper to the effect that she would be prepared to exchange her house in the South of France – central heating, use of car, two bedrooms, sleeps twelve at a pinch – for similar accommodation in London for a period of four weeks.

A Mrs Stifflewood rang almost immediately, expressing her interest, from a swish Chelsea address, and offering the use of *her* car, on the grounds that London taxis were so expensive, plus her telephone number, together with the assurance that she had neither children nor other destructive encumbrances. Furthermore, she wished to be assured that Mrs Murple's house was well isolated, because she was in urgent need of peace and quiet.

'Well,' Mrs Murple told us, 'I called her back and got ever such an angry man on the phone who said that no Mrs Stifflewood lived there, that he had never heard of Mrs Stifflewood and that she'd just got him out of his bath.' Mrs Murple made an addendum. 'I mean *I'd* just got him out of his bath because, of course, Mrs Stifflewood wasn't there.'

We were digesting this somewhat tangled spaghetti when Mrs Murple said, 'Imagine if we'd gone to London with all our luggage and arrived at Mrs Stifflewood's house only to find that she wasn't there but that where she really was was at the back door of our isolated house loading every single thing we owned into an enormous furniture van and then selling all our lovely things to some awful antique dealer in Nice.'

I liked it. It had the stamp of good planning but not, I thought a moment later, quite good enough.

For a start, Mrs Stifflewood should not have given the address and telephone number of the man in the bath but simply the number of a public call-box convenient to her place of residence – conceivably a lodging house in the Seven Dials area. In this way there would be a fair chance of the number being engaged, or providing no reply, every time Mrs Murple rang. This would have to suggest to Mrs Murple that Mrs Stifflewood lived a life of intense activity, either social or commercial, and should therefore be a person of standing.

The other mistake that Mrs Stifflewood had made, in my view, was not finding out enough about Mrs Murple's goodies. After all, if two ladies are about to exchange houses it would not be in the nature of either of them to allow that one had the edge on the other. The conversation should have gone like this:

Mrs Stifflewood (notebook in hand): 'I've got a dear little upright piano. I'm sure you'll take good care of it.'

Mrs Murple (delighted): 'Oh, you play too! I've had my concert grand for centuries. It's such a relief after the television and all my husband's enormous stereophonic stuff. He's got masses of it.'

Mrs Stifflewood (writing busily): 'I've a few little bits of silver, but my maid does all the polishing.'

Mrs Murple (radiant): 'I do all my own. My mother left me some of the most beautiful Georgian stuff you've ever seen. Of course, I could put it away – save you the trouble.'

Mrs Stifflewood (her mouth watering): 'No, no, I assure you. No trouble at all . . .'

I've still got a few little things to work out,

like how to get Mrs Murple to pay for the hire of Mrs Stifflewood's pantechnicon, plus her first-class return air-fare London-Nice-London, but all that will come in time.

In the interval I'm going to have the pleasure of reading the Exchange Accommodation advertisements with an entirely fresh eye.

Ann Dumme – meet Anne Derr

'But of course we know them,' cried the lady, abandoning Tiggy and Boko without, apparently, another thought. Proving her point up to the hilt she said, 'We've known them simply for centuries. Mary and um dear old Lobbity.'

It was the worst possible luck. I had asked her if she knew these two unspeakables to divert her – permanently if possible – from the subject of Tiggy and Boko, a couple of Pekinese, and now found that she did – to the extent of calling the purple-faced Lawrence 'dear old Lobbity'. The future became even darker than it had been a moment before.

'Actually,' said the lady, 'talking about Mary and Lobbity absolutely the funniest thing happened with them last Tuesday and um—'

Having established with 'and um' that she was still in mid-speech, she paused to light a cigarette. This task completed, none too tidily, she resumed at the same place. 'And um actually Tiggy and Boko were all mixed up in it as well.'

She blew a lot of smoke into my face, marshalling her thoughts. I could hear them clicking, in a tinny way.

'You see,' she said, now feeling confident about her opening and the next, say, two thousand words, 'Mary asked us to lunch and um we hadn't seen them for ages so I simply had to have my hair done and um at the very same time silly old Vernon decides he's got to take Tiggy to the vet. I told you,' she said, with a hint of accusation, in case I'd forgotten, 'about poor Tig's back legs—'

She waited for me to nod before proceeding. 'So of course the vet's absolutely in one direction and um my hairdresser is in exactly the other and you know what Vernon is like about making up his mind so the upshot of it is that I have to take a taxi and um—'

I slipped my ears into neutral, coasting along on the clattering flood of sound. None-theless, something was still nagging at me. This 'and um' business – surely one of the most enraging social usages of all time.

The 'and ummers' do it either to indicate that they haven't nearly finished, and there-fore require no interruption, or simply because they have no idea what they are going to say next and wish to remain in the driving seat until the motor begins to turn over again and um—

Then, in a single, incandescent flash, I saw her. Ann Dumme. Ann Dumme, hanging around at parties all these years waiting to be introduced or for someone to include her in a coherent way, just for once, in the conversation.

Ann Dumme, rather large, nearly thirty, daughter, unmarried, of Colonel Alaistair Dumme – 'Dummy', affectionately, to his brother officers and 'Dummy', frankly, to his men.

Poor Ann Dumme, in a difficult yellow dress, starting forwards slightly as her name is mentioned yet again and then falling back in confusion as the talk swings wildly, confusingly away from her.

'Ann Dumme, Tiggy and Boko were all mixed up in it as well.'

Ann cannot understand it. She's never heard of Tiggy or Boko or, if it comes to that, Mary Ann Dumme or dear old Lobbity. There she is right in the middle of it again, without even a comma to separate her from two total strangers.

I feel passionately for poor Ann Dumme, always a subject for conversation but never, as it were a bride . . .

'And er there's silly old Vernon with a puncture and Tiggy wants to go pee-pees and er—'

My God, another one. Anne Derr. But

quite a different kettle of fish to unhappy, unmarried Ann Dumme.

Anne Derr is very very thin and very very smart, a vodka drinker with a head like an anvil, married – her fourth husband – to Bernard Derr, a stockbroker who's managed, despite recent difficulties, to hang on to not only seven race horses but also his yacht.

The exceedingly elegant Anne Derr isn't in the least surprised that her name is on every tongue, constantly. She doesn't bother to listen to what the silly bitches are saying about her. It's enough that she should be conversational subject Number One. Ann Dumme watches her namesake wistfully, wishing she could smoke small, thin cigars like Anne Derr . . .

'So by this time, of course, dopey Vernon is on the phone to Carlo who's just doing the difficult bit round the back of my neck—'

'Ann Dumme,' I said. 'Anne Derr.'

'And er,' said the lady, thankful to be so ably prompted, 'what was I supposed to do when Carlo simply cannot be disturbed at a time like . . .'

I slipped my ears back into neutral and went coasting along again, nursing a dear little secret of my own.

Two babies over Pa

Feeling like Merlin, with a somewhat bent wand, I stepped out on to Biot golf-course for the first time in a year to see what miracles might be wrought not with the full bag of tools but with a single club.

As usual it was John Langley, on his annual visit to the South of France, who tempted me into the arena with the suggestion that a few holes up and down the flatter pastures of Biot, armed only with a five-iron, might be better for us than several other things we might do instead.

I found an immediate sense of freedom about this simplified game. No caddy, whose experienced eye tells him, after the first two holes, that his present patron will get one off the middle of the stick only by accident and not too often at that, so that he settles into that mood of discontent which would certainly do him out of a tip if the player had the unthinkable courage to withhold it.

None of that choice, for one simple shot, between three irons, excluding the one presented by the caddy who, if he be engaged in the matter at all, can only be expecting a miracle. Really just a succession of light-hearted blows with one stick terminating, eventually, on the green, where a five-iron bounces in putts of fifteen feet which would certainly turn into three if played with a putter.

John and I did rather well. The core of the beautiful swing with which he led the Walker Cup team was still there whilst I, becoming accustomed to the vagaries of only one club, managed to straighten out, in part, the high, looping, left-handed banana shot that has been the mainstay of my game since 1927. Then, without warning of any kind, we suddenly saw the most extraordinary thing we had ever seen on any golf-course, any-where in the world. A man playing golf with a child on his back.

That is, having been ridden by the child to the next tee, right up there on his shoulders, he would dismount the nipper, prop it up against his caddy cart, have a slash with his driver, upsadaisy with the baby and off to where the drive had come to rest, not too far away. And not only this but we actually saw him hole a three-foot putt, with the child on his shoulders, gripping on to his ears.

When we got in we had a long talk about this phenomenon, in the bar. It seemed a matter deserving of discussion in depth.

I drove off with the promise that if you are on a golfcourse, wanting to play golf, but accoutred not only with a full set of clubs but also a small child, it would surely be more rational to have a pram than a caddy-cart for the transport of the accessories. In this way you would not have the surely tiring duty of hoisting the child up and down in between shots, with the additional hazards of crying or the child being excused while you are looking for a ball in long, already damp grass.

'Ah,' John said, 'but he slotted in that tricky little three-footer with the child up.'

It was from this point that the discussion flowered into the possibilities of playing golf not with a full bag of clubs but with a full pram, the contents to be worn by selection.

Say, now, we said, you had a five-iron and a choice of, perhaps, six children, ranging from a year to four years and therefore of varying weights and disposition. For simplicity's sake, rather than limit ourselves to the old nomenclature of driver, two-wood, three-iron, wedge, etc., we decided to call our pramful of – as it were – clubs by human names, like Timmy, Charlie, Freddie, Alice and fat Caroline.

'If,' said John, who knows a lot about golf, 'if I was faced with a punchy five-iron into the teeth of a bitterly cold east wind I'd pick that Caroline out of the pram and wrap her around my neck. With all that weight she'd keep you right down, squarely all the way through the ball – and nice and warm.'

'Very true,' I said. 'Good for you. But listen. You can easily envisage the impossibility, out of a hanging lie, of chopping up a five-iron over a pot bunker one hundred yards ahead of you and getting it to bite on a green that's running all the way away to the left. That's one for that malicious little rat Alice. Seeing that the shot is simply not on to begin with and will almost inevitably lead to a shank off the pipe all the blame can be laid, fairly and squarely, on that pinching and hair pulling that is regarded by Alice as fun.'

We were ranging over the prehensile legs of lanky little Charlie as an aide to a full pivot on a big, booming five-iron down-wind when John stopped us stone dead. 'Who's going to push the pram?' he said. 'With five or six clubs in there you're going to have a lot of meat.' 'Plus,' I agreed, 'plenty of stuff like milk, fruit-cake and gobstoppers, to keep them up to scratch.'

We settled in the end for two *au pair* girls, a dark Dane, a blonde Swede. One each.

All square at the end of the match, after we'd stashed away the pram.

Super spats for swimming

Everyone will tell you – hundreds of them, including those who can't do it – that of all therapeutic measures for the alleviation of almost any ailment known to, and baffling, medical science swimming is the absolute top.

Swimming, they will assure you with powerful authority, will straighten out curvature of the spine, remove varicose veins, re-knit an Achilles heel, dissolve warts, replace the heart with a new one – in a word, or two, swimming will cure whatever you've got without leaving the slightest trace of scar tissue. Just get into a piece of clean sea – the lagoon of a desert island? – or a properly medicated pool – someone else's? – swim around for a while and spring out of the water wholly renewed in wind, limb and brain. Swimming, in fact, will beat a course of injections into a cocked hat.

I'm sure it would, if you can swim. I mean, swim properly, as opposed to the feeble flapping or frantic thrashing which is the lot of those of us who have never learned this arcane trick.

It's all mixed up with the feet. Get the feet – as far as I can make out – buzzing up and down and you're one hundred yards away before you've had time to fit in more than three or four scoopings with the arms.

It's a pedal movement as complex and as dependent upon timing as tap dancing although, admittedly, more limited in bucks, wings and other variations. But, just like tap dancing, it's the first step, as it were, that counts.

Have I not spent many an hour, semi-submerged, holding on to a piece of drift-wood or a rubber ring, trying to get that magic foot-buzzing going only to find it drawing me, very slowly, backwards until the other, unwanted, end of the pool brings the exercise to a halt, often painfully

So I throw away my truss, or crutch, fill both lungs with as much air as they will take, and slash out on my own, hoping to reach if not the other end at least the shallow bit that precedes it. Of course, I've never seen myself swimming but I fancy I've got not a half-bad Johnny Weissmuller (rtd) arm action, reaching rhythmically and powerfully forward, but it's the nonsense going on at the other end that makes me sick. That, and the twisted spout that appears under my left arm, sucking desperately for air and getting one hundred and three per cent water.

The potential propeller at the other end seems better designed for the beating of something enormous like ostrich eggs. A kind of sideways frog kick, as the left arm curves most beautifully forward, but followed by an aimless and, indeed, destructive battering of the feet as the right arm, much shorter in throw, tries to keep the craft under way. I arrive at the other end ship-wrecked, gasping, water-logged and blind, far removed from being improved in health and, indeed, in some doubt about continued survival.

I got Swimming Tom to come and have a look at this stuff, in the hope that he could bodge up a mod. Tom fell, pushed, into his swimming team at school and has been a non-competing swimming expert ever since. He said I was doing 'the trudgen' and left it at that, apparently envisaging no worthwhile repairs.

Having known the word for years I looked it up in the dictionary and found that 'trudgen' was 'swimming with alternate right & left over-arm strokes & *ordinary* leg action'. The italics are mine, without further comment.

I can't imagine, after that set-back, why I went on thinking about swimming but I did and suddenly my mind was bursting with waterwings, fully inflated. Not back-wings, nor arm-wings but *ankle*-wings, surely, up till now, unknown in the world of aquatics.

I got to ankle-wings by way of the arm-wings I'd once seen on a *cocotte* taking her ease in the sea in Cannes. She must have been all of three years of age, wearing – pointlessly

– a bikini, a 1932 hair perm and these absolutely fab arm-wings. But what arm-wings. None of that bloated red rubber you might see on the *plage* at East Wittering, but ruched, lacey creations almost resembling pouffed sleeves, obviously her mother's plan to keep that divine hair out of the water.

What about a pair of those around my ankles, the feet – with the weight taken off them – thrashing away like an electric blender! Some speed.

Then I ran into a technical problem. Who, when they were on and out of my range, was going to blow them up?

Something even more awkward occurred to me. Say, wearing my super-spats, I had perforce minced into the sea off the Carlton beach, struck out with the threshers going like mad, suffered a simultaneous puncture in both of them and rammed the jetty, head-on, like a torpedo, the concussion hurling Sophia Loren into the sea on the other side.

There's more in swimming than you think.

Gammon's back

We might be sitting around, four or five of us, after lunch or dinner or both, the two functions having welded themselves into a continuous and, by the look of it, an immovable feast, and we are all in expansive mood, discussing the frailties of happily absent best friends, delivering political opinions which are given some weight at least by repetition, even a couple of us working in close harmony on *Nellie Dean*.

But there is something rotten in this otherwise swinging *soirée*. Two members of the gathering are hunched in a distant corner over a small table bent upon some game involving dice, which rattle with the exuberance of small bones in an old graveyard. As far as we are concerned the players themselves could be equally dead except that the silence of their graves is broken by hoarse cries of either triumph or abuse, at mercifully infrequent intervals, because we do not wish to be reminded in any way of their presence.

They are, of course, playing backgammon, the swiftest and deadliest killjoy that social life has ever known. Make no mistake on this one. I've got nothing against backgammon *per se*. I only want it to be played in another room or a club or a padded cell so that it cannot lay its cool hand on general conversation, or – and this is its most poisonous influence – draw others away from the merry fireside to watch it at close range, yielding within minutes to the temptation to give hare-brained advice to either or both players who may, quite possibly, be playing it very badly anyway.

I'm going to come clean here. That's how I began, only last week, to play backgammon itself. Having listened to it or actually watched it being played for some time, I decided the hour had come to blood myself, having admittedly but a slender hold on the rules or tactics of the game. 'All right, Sandy,' I said, 'I'll take you on. But the very last thing I want is a single word of advice. I want to learn this thing the hard way.'

'Great,' Sandy said. 'You set up the board.'

Five rather rattled minutes later, after I'd distributed the counters in what looked like select groups, I said, 'That about right?'

'Very nearly,' Sandy said. 'But if I may just—' He repositioned about fifty per cent of the counters. I noticed the knuckles on his hand were curiously white. Pointing, he said, 'That's your inner table, your outer table, your bar point—'

'Let's just play,' I said.

We each threw one die – a six for me and a one for Sandy.

'Great throw,' he said. 'Right into your bar point.'

'You mean it's my turn?'

'Sure.'

'I can add those numbers together?'

'Sure. But it wouldn't be very—'

'No advice, please,' I snapped. I picked up one of my counters and to relieve the tension – mine – I began counting, in a Dublin accent, 'Wan tuw tree fower fiev six sivin,' and slammed my man down into a new hole.

After a moment – he seemed to be under some pressure – Sandy said, 'I'm very sorry, but you're going the wrong way.'

'Am I? All right. May I put it back?'

'Do.' He sat forward a little. 'May I just point out that when you begin counting wan – I mean, one – you begin not from the point you're on but from the next wan – one.'

'I see. Thank you.'

The game, after only one throw of two dice, seemed to have fallen into a state incapable of advancement.

Sandy, obviously eager for a little more action, said, 'May I just show you how to make your bar point?'

'Do.'

He did so, just by movement, without counting aloud. I made a mental note. In the next game – if there was going to be one – if I threw a six and Sandy a one I knew what my first move would be. 'Right,' I said. 'Let's get cracking.'

Sandy threw a double six and moved handfuls of men like lightning, double me – whatever that was – and finally gammoned me – whatever that might have been.

I have an obscene confession to make. There is now a brandnew backgammon set in our very own house. Madame and I have occasional little games that get into entanglements, every time, that would take Sandy more than an hour to straighten out.

Despite a lot of practice I'm still keeping my heaviest shot in my locker. 'Wan tuw tree fower fiev . . . ,' beginning from one point too soon.

I find it creates passions in more skilful players that bring us right back to those vivacious nights around the fire.

Bleeding blue blood

I haven't done anything about it since my father died and my blood turned blue and I became Lord Glenavy, for the reason, I suppose, that it needs work if one is to get any mileage out of being a Baron.

A Baron, for instance, if he's going to be a

real one, is expected to take his seat in the House of Lords. There's a roll of drums, or something and Black rod – or it might be Gold Stick – opens the door and the new peer marches up to the Woolsack wearing a cloak and carrying a kind of crown and then he turns round twice and bows to the Lord Chancellor and says something on the lines of. 'I swear eternal loyalty and obedience to—' but even in my imagination I can never get beyond, 'I swear—'

That is not true. I can get as far as, 'I—' and then everything shuts down, because not even in the dock, in the presence of armed police, can I say, 'I swear—', since my stammer cuts me off, in toto, from pronouncing any word that begins with 'sw'. The police and the judge and the jury are prepared to wait, on the grounds that they cannot get on with the business of hanging me, or whatever else they may have in mind, until I've said, 'I swear by Almighty God—', but I've always pictured the House of Lords as being too busy with its own affairs to be prepared to sit there all day long waiting for the new member to get past the second word of the Oath, with God knows what further problems to come, later on.

The device of wearing a bowler hat and saying, 'I affirm—' seems too strained to be worth attention.

I have, however, attended the House of Lords when I was only an Honourable, blood medium blue. The Lord St Oswald, I think it was, told me that the eldest sons of peers had the privilege of sitting on the steps of the Throne and I thought that surely must be good enough for the *Sunday Dispatch*, for which I was writing a column at the time.

It was worth a guinea a minute from the word go. Arrival outside the Chamber in a Mini Traveller, royal blue, and pounced upon instantly by an enormous policeman who said that only lords could leave their vehicles in this particular area. 'But, officer,' I said, 'I'm the eldest son of a peer.' Instantly, the old Jack Warner salute, deferential but twinkly smile and, 'I do beg your pardon, sir – just in beside that dark-green Rolls.'

Same again inside. Leaped upon by two men dressed as head waiters, with the addition of large gold medallions dangling down to their knees – 'Public Gallery to the left, sir.' I let it slip about being the eldest son of a peer and they practically carried me into the ante-chamber where the Lords Attlee and Longford – the one before he achieved notoriety and the other having had it – were signing a sort of Visitors' Book. I scratched my moniker below theirs and was shown into the Chamber by an assistant who was kind enough to dismantle a brass (gold?) rail which stood between me and the Steps of the Throne, and to re-erect it when I was safely inside.

It was lonely in there, in the absence of the Queen or the Duke of Edinburgh. The Steps of the Throne were shallow and hard, up-holstered in a not very flash bit of red drugget. I arranged 6 ft 5 of myself on a number of them, looking like something from the bad end of the Bowery, and placed a finger on the side of my face, in thinking posture.

Some disturbance was evident among the Conservative peers. Quite a few of them leant across to their neighbour, and I could see their lips forming the words, 'Christ, what's that? Surely not one of ours?' The Labour lords, on the other hand, didn't give a damn, being for the most part only imitation blue.

The late Lord Esher was talking to us about the need for more common land for cows to eat off and after half an hour I left him to it. Outside, I asked the rail-dismantling assistant how he knew I was the eldest son of a peer and he replied instantly, 'One recognizes the family likeness, sir,' which showed he must have been as quick as a whippet in this department seeing that my father took his seat, in which he never sat, in three minutes dead, wearing blue glasses and with his coat collar turned up, in fear of being shot for disloyalty, on his immediate return to Dublin, by the IRA.

Outside, I asked the car-park policeman why *he* had accepted my statement that I was the eldest son of a peer, and with a really superb Jack Warner twinkle he said, 'Well, sir, there wouldn't be much percentage in being an imposter in *there*.'

The piece never appeared in the *Sunday Dispatch*. Someone said that Lord Rothermere thought it was disrespectful, though God knows what he thought he was doing reading it at all.

The blueness of my blood, which has been blue now for about twelve years, comes from the village of Glenavy, in the North of Ireland. I once did a programme about blue blood for Ulster Television, in Belfast, sharing the bill with the Duke and Duchess of Bedford, and in order to jazz up the modest proceedings they sent a two-man film unit to the village beforehand to garner the views of the natives about their absentee squire. Not a single one of them had ever heard of me. Nor did they know that the name of their village had been filched. The piece of information they were lacking was, of course, that my great-great-grandfather was the local police-man and had risen to the rank of sergeant after being an absolute swine for years and years, but they couldn't know that because I hadn't told the producer, thinking it would embarrass the Bedfords if the matter came to light.

I am, in fact, pure police blue, and you can't have it bluer than that.

Night, all. Mind how you go.

AFOTF-4

At Home Abroad

Tarte au ciment

I always feel it's such a comfort to be well-known in a restaurant.

Wait! Let me correct that, before nausea spreads.

I don't mean that it's such a comfort to be well-kown and then go into a restaurant, being well-kown all over it. I'm trying to say that it's nice to be pretty well-known to nearly all the waiters in three or four restaurants to which one goes fairly regularly – say, about once a month. Not pretty well-known, of course, as a big spender who gives tips so lavish that he can only have left all the rest of his money, inadvertently, behind, but merely as a reliable customer who doesn't often break glasses, complain or ring to book a table for four at eight o'clock and turn up at 9.30 with seven, five of whom are already far from sober.

A reliable customer of this kind can win a number of advantages. He can be spared the obviously most desirable table in the window – desirable, that is, until the next customer comes in, throws the door open against the back of one's chair, leaving it slightly ajar so that an east wind can get in, too. Or the cosy table well away from draughts and kitchen uproar but perhaps just a shade too close to the cloakroom, so that many people, divesting themselves for dinner, dangle heavy overcoats into your *Porc Braisé aux Choux Rouges*, or whatever else one might be trying to munch.

All these comforts, including unvarying agreement about the wine list. Not the rhubarb juice in the carafe, but the slightly more expensive stuff in the bottle which the waiter puts on the table by habit, rather than by request. If you've got a good connection going he almost knows what you're going to eat before you've asked for it, saving you the trouble of ploughing through what we've both come to know as 'the race card'. A special language of this kind takes a lot of the agony out of ordering, lending lunch or dinner a welcome ambience of genial fun.

When I lived in Dublin, years ago, and patronized Jammet's Restaurant, being the only one in the entire city of French origin, my order to Paddy (no relation), the old waiter with the curling cardboard dicky, was always the same. 'Slash the knuckles off a couple of sheep's legs and then ice cream with a drop of the proprietor's blood.' On the very first occasion Paddy knew what I was talking about. Red grenadine sauce on the ice, much easier to come by than a drop of Louis Jammet's blood, a stern Frenchman who, in his many years in Dublin, never gave a single customer one free drink. He and his restaurant are long since gone, but their memory lingers on, so tenderly, indeed, that it led me into *Tarte au Ciment*, now that we live in France, and know quite a lot of cheerful little *bistrots*.

In these small family restaurants the dessert is almost always *Tarte aux Pommes* – sliced apples on a base of pastry so solid that it's clear they've been purchased from a factory, rather than lovingly made by hand on the premises. It is for this reason, while eating out, that I always refer to *Tarte aux Pommes* as *Tarte aux Ciment* when we get to this stage of the repast, and many a waiter knows exactly what I mean.

Well, then, the other day we had lunch in Tourettes with Peter and Philip and Nola in a small place almost beside their own, it being closed on Mondays and Thursdays. No rivalry between the two establishments. Warm welcome from a very pretty girl. Lovely lunch and we came to the dessert. '*Pour moi*', I said to her – we had a good connection going – '*la Tarte au Ciment*'. Gravely, she noted it down and came back with the oddest looking *tarte* I'd ever seen. More like a block of pale-mauve ice cream, decorated with a small purple flower and two strips of stuff resembling frozen *crème caramele*. I looked at it steadily for a moment. Whatever it was it had pastry underneath it. Undeniably a *tarte*, but made of what. I shovelled a large forkful into my mouth and, of course, it was cement. Cement delicately blended with fine sand. And the purple flower was made of paper and the little strips of stuff were tiles.

With a mouthful of cement I couldn't speak. Didn't know what to do. Nola, sitting opposite me, said, 'What's wrong – isn't it good?' – and helped herself with a teaspoon from my plate. We were both turned to stone. The chef-proprietor appeared, his huge moustache dripping with tears of laughter. Holding on to the wall he said to Madame, 'Is he angry?' 'He can't speak yet,' she replied, 'so I don't know.'

Nola and I scoured our mouths with handkerchiefs, napkins, corners of the tablecloth, every crevice in our teeth packed with cement and sand. We got it all out, after a most unusual struggle, and bravely washed the remnants away with wine.

I shall not be making the same joke again.

Imperfect peace

Last Sabbath day Lord Darby and Lady Joan arose not too promptly and after some not very effective scratching around decided to halt all further activity in favour of lying in long chairs under umbrellas in the garden, books and gentle refreshment to hand, the Golden Oldies being a little vertiginous after the social whirlings of the Young Visitor, who had just left after two weeks of laying waste to the countryside.

The cicada gave us about ten minutes of sabbatical peace and then began rubbing his back legs together, or whatever these ghastly grasshoppers do to make their intolerable noise. They live invisibly in the olive trees. Suddenly, they decide to make their presence known, presumably to other creatures of the same species, by making this noise that sounds exactly like a very old pram, with squeaky, ovoid wheels, being pushed with unimaginable urgency uphill.

After a short spell of this nerve-grating uproar I got the spade from the potting shed, tracked down the tree and beat the trunk as though it were an Orange drum. Either this frightens the cicada into silence or the vibration knots its back legs together. In any case, peace drifted gently over us again – for three minutes, until the holiday car came carousing up the hill.

It was easy to tell it was a holiday car, having successfully negotiated the lethal autoroute from Paris, because the litter in its roof-rack – deckchairs, deflated dinghies, roped suitcases – was visible above the hedge, and the radio was playing at full blast. It turned – of course – into the house on the other side of the road and from it there debouched, by the sound of their voices, three elderly women, one youngish man, four small children and two dogs. The women had voices like corrugated iron being beaten with a hammer. The youngish man was basso profundo, in a fury, whilst the children's contribution to the din put one in mind of huge wild mice. The dogs began to bark – Alsatians, by the demented ferocity of their booming. The cicada started up again, not to be outdone by strangers from the north.

Everything settled down, then, to straight pandemonium. The new arrivals began to lay the table for lunch, apparently by throwing plates on to a tin surface from the range of six feet, shouting at one another in obvious good-humour. Two of the children cried piercingly whilst the other two sang loudly, but not very well. The dogs went on barking, probably frightened by worms – something well outside their urban experience. The cicada thrashed its back legs into a blur.

We lay there, holding on to the sides of our long chairs, knowing only too well, now, what had happened. This Sabbath day was the first of August, the very day on which the whole population of France moves south, with the impact of the world's biggest travelling circus, to thrash and bang around these parts until the thirty-first of August, when they load up, as one man, for their return, leaving a riven world behind.

By 3.30 p.m. we thought the uproar had reached its apogee. The holiday-makers opposite were far gone in wine. The Alsatians, terrified even by leaves, had started off all the other visiting dogs, on both side of the valley, in addition to the resident ones, in vigorous competition. The four children had filled their inflatable dinghy with water and were using it as a screaming pool. And then the man down the road started boring holes in what sounded like sheet steel, with an electric drill.

The trouble is that around here, in the month of August, too many people rent their houses to too many summer visitors. With the prohibitive proceeds they probably go scurrying off to London, to buy ton after ton of underwear in Oxford street, in lovely devalued pounds. One would imagine that the summer visitors come here for the pleasures of the beach, and so do they, until they find that there is standing-room only, even on the rocks, between Menton and Perpignan. This decides them to stay in their rented homes, there to divert themselves as best they can, often by doing small jobs, like boring holes in steel plating – and cutting logs with mechanical saws.

This last intrusion was beyond belief. This young man, with his father to feed in the logs, started his petrol-engined saw at 3.35 p.m., and sawed away until six o'clock. A petrol-engined saw screeches at the smaller logs and snarls at the larger ones. It sounds like a drill big enough and angry enough to make holes in the teeth of King Kong. But not loud enough to drown the sound of the music.

The music came booming down the hill, an uproar that suggested a whole orchestra quarry-blasting away at one of the works of Wagner. Conducted, as usual, from his balcony by the small man with the silvery hair who comes here every summer to give us the benefit of his stereophonics.

Roll on, sweet, gentle September, roll on.

Red Duster in rubies

We were sitting on the blunt end of this motor-cruiser which, if I hadn't been so lazy, I could probably have bought for, say, £250,000, looking at the other thing in the next berth but one.

Port Canto, naturally, in Cannes, where the thunder of rattling banknotes drowns the roar of marine engines, many of them gold-plated, prettily picked out in platinum, with diamond knobs. Byzantium on sea really, but for all the cruising the majority of these palaces engage in they might just as well be on land, after adaptation of the plumbing.

Once saw two elderly English couples in Monte Carlo harbour, under an awning – looked as if it was made of pure silk – on the afterdeck playing Bridge, attended by *three* stewards in *white* gloves, encumbered in their services by a thousand gladioli, seven feet high, in a gold bucket. That kind of thrashing into a nasty north-easter, with the bilges slopping over your feet and the port-side engine on the blink, with scurvy rife aboard.

This thing we were looking at, in the next berth but one, had some of the feeling of a minaret made of precious metals right down to the basement. It glowed with money, in the sun. A curious kind of beigy-greeny establishment, with immense, peach-coloured windows curving round the after-drawing-room. A mast in the form of a towering, thin triangle all knobbly with electronic instruments of massive size, including television cameras to keep eternal vigilance on every single inch of the boat, both in and out.

High up in the sharp end this minaret of precious metals has a swimming-pool, just below the bridge. No doubt there are tanks below to fill the pool with rose water, or ass's milk, according to whim. Far below the waterline is a laundry, the size of a laundry, so that everyone can have clean sheets every hour, on the hour, including the ship's cat, if any.

Lined up discreetly on the quay, side by side, were two 600 Mercedes limousines, those locomotives which are so long that they can accommodate four back doors, and often do. One of them was black and the other pale chocolate, and behind the wheel of each of them sat a chauffeur, all day long, in case anyone wanted to travel three hundred yards to buy a box of matches. As an adjunct to these limousines, but not in attendance at the moment, is a Rolls Royce Camargue, together with a kennel of Cadillacs – just fun cars, really. To say nothing – because what can one say? – of two private Boeing 707's, one of which was probably in Moscow at this very moment, picking up a little more caviar.

In addition to these possessions there is also a second yacht, to serve as an annexe for guests who are only mono-millionaires. Neither of them, of course, is as big as the German yacht, moored at the end of the wall. The German yacht is the owner's second helping. The first one struck a rock and sank, during her sea trials. The owner put in an immediate order for another one, but rather larger in size, all over. There is presumably no animosity between the two owners. One boat may be bigger than the other one, but if you put two together they're going to be bigger still, so we're kind of all-square.

The owner of the minaret now appears on the after sundeck, in consultation, probably about business rather than flower arrangement or Schopenhauer, with three gentlemen who appear nervous, if not frightened into the gibbering screaming-meemies. There is a bar up there, attended day and night by relays of stewards, but the owner appears to abstain from refreshment. After all, he's only got to put his hand out to find a glass in it and he's probably sick of it.

The conference breaks up and everyone disappears below, possibly for a game of snooker in the billiard room or to watch the Olympics in the private theatre, cinema-sized television screen, natch, and at this moment a taxi arrives with two trembling executives in pin-striped suits. It is clear that they've just flown in from London, because both of them carry plastic bags of duty-free booze, a hopeless gift to the minaret. They also pay for their own taxi, watched with profound disdain by the chauffeurs in giant Mercedes, both of whom could easily have gone to the airport and given the new arrivals a free limousine each.

The new arrivals, sweating in their heavy pin-stripe suits, appear on the after deck and give the barman their bottles, who looks at them as if they were some kind of disinfectant and then gives them a proper drink.

The two pin-stripers pace up and down like caged lions, or frightened wolves, awaiting the appearance of the owner.

It is significant that the Red Duster droops in the breathless heat from the minaret's stern.

In Port Canto the Red Duster is now a flag of convenience, about as convenient as Liberia.

Evader with tomato

'Where's the best place – really the best place – to watch all the battle-ships from?' The young man was disturbingly eager. And so was his even younger wife. 'We thought we could sort of have lunch at one of those little beach restaurants and see it all from there.'

'Which little beach restaurant?' I enquired. 'And where?'

'Well, we thought you'd know which would be the best one. Not too far away, of course. You could come in our car.'

Obviously, they had sensed a degree of opposition in the air, and were trying to dilute it. The young man played a card that looked to him like an ace. 'Lunch would be on us, of course.'

'Very kind,' I said. 'But the ironic thing is that while the French navy has the whole of the Mediterranean to float on, excluding naturally enough those portions occupied by the Russians and the Americans, we have not had a drop of water in our house for thirty-six hours.'

The young man was puzzled by the connection. 'Oh,' he said, 'I see.' He looked at his wife, to see if she saw more than he did, but appeared disappointed. 'But that wouldn't matter,' he said, 'if we were lunching out.'

'One of the very few people to be lunching today, anywhere near Nice, will be Giscard d'Estaing, aboard the aircraft carrier *Clemenceau*. Everyone else will be standing on the neck of everyone else. They estimate,' I went on, hammering in the nails, 'that there are going to be 200,000 people on the Promenade des Anglais alone, and another 500,000 in the back streets of Nice, trying to find somewhere to leave their cars. All,' I said gently, 'for the purpose of watching twenty-seven French warships proceed from Villefranche to Toulon ten miles off-shore in a sea mist which will render them invisible. I, personally, would be far better employed here watching our water.'

The young man was tiring. 'What's wrong with your water?' he said, rather roughly.

'There's a rumour that a bulldozer tore up the main water pipe in Bar-sur-Loup. They've been trying, all day and all night, to mend it, without success.' I went on to explain, in detail, what would happen, in all probability, when the water eventually came through. 'Fearful pressure, air-locks, taps blown off the wall, general inundation—' About half-way through this dissertation the great French naval review sank without a trace, as a source of entertaiment. They spent the day sitting somewhat disconsolately round the

105

garden, in cloudy, humid weather.

Next morning we still had no water, but just in case it did arrive, without subsequent flooding, I had another substantial arrow in my quiver. I let it fly, giving my car to the garage for a two-day service, thereby removing me from any possibility of having to drive them to the grand parade of the jazz – Count Basie and Dizzy Gillespie – in the Jardins de Cimiez, once again back in Nice, probably still littered with the aftermath of the naval review.

Furthermore, I had another, unexpected, bonus. All day long it had been trying to rain and, from time to time, succeeding.

'Pity about the rain,' I said. 'We'd never get the four of us, our picnic dinner and the two big umbrellas, with their cast-iron bases, into your Mini.'

The young people, who had come down specifically for the jazz festival, with the naval review as an additional thrill, began to detect a familiar opacity in the air. He said, 'But we've got our macs.'

'Unfortunately,' I said, 'I keep mine in London.'

'But,' the girl said, 'we don't really have to bother about dinner.'

'On the other hand,' I said, 'you're going to be there for hours, in the open air, listening to a load of junk whilst you're waiting for Basie and Dizzy. That's not going to be much fun in heavy rain.'

Suddenly, Madame said, 'Well, the three of us are going, anyway. I imagine you'll be all right by yourself.'

This was as far as was conceivably possible from my original plan, which had been a jolly little dinner for four, cooked by Madame – the water had mercifully come back again – and I enjoying a new audience for my somewhat threadbare anecdotage. They left and I went to bed with a tomato.

The young people left early, and thankfully, the following morning. And I discovered that the next day was July the fourteenth, Bastille Day, a general holiday in France, and the post office shut. That's why, still deprived of my car, I had to walk two miles downhill, and ten miles back on Tuesday, the thirteenth of July.

This is the season for the summer visitor. Pity one can't win 'em all.

Villains on vacation

During the recent Easter break the teaming villains of the Côte d'Azur would seem to have turned from the heavier side of their industry, i.e.: gang murder, drug smuggling, arson and the protection racket, to the lighter and more relaxing craft of burglary, presumably on the grounds that everyone, and they in particular, are entitled to a short holiday after the rigours of winter.

They were certainly relaxing into any number of houses down here.

A friend, arriving to spend a happy Easter at his newly redecorated house in Beaulieu, found to his surprise that the job had actually been completed. Almost immediately after that, however, he became aware that the house looked curiously empty, which it was. Some team of experts had removed the furnishings and the appointments in their entirety, down to and including three old egg-spoons, and – even as our friend arrived – were conducting an open-air auction of same on the building site next door – or so our friend suspected, identifying with some certainty a number of his larger pieces, as they were driven away. He rang the police without delay. They asked if he was insured. He said he was always careful in matters of that kind. They said that that was good and that they would try to get round within the next few days.

On Easter Saturday the same or, more probably, an allied group, broke into the home of a Parisian gentleman who has a secondary residence in our village and, as in the previous case, stripped it down to the egg-spoons, almost certainly using a furniture van. Then, having a few bits and pieces left over, they loaded them into the automobile belonging to the Parisian gentleman's cousin, who lives next door, and drove it away, too. Without doubt they would have had the Parisian gentleman's automobile as well, had he not been sitting in it in the village, five minutes away, while his wife did some shopping. We all agreed that she would have bought more, had she known what awaited her return.

That very afternoon another friend of ours arrived from London with one Burmese cat, one Siamese cat and one fourteen-year-old son, to take up permanent residence in a house just down the road. He was absolutely delighted to find the plumber actually upon the matter of by-passing the old-fashioned pump which had supplied water to the household for many years. It seemed to be an exceedingly happy omen in view of the fact that the by-passing of the pump had first been mooted in 1968, when the plumber said he would start tomorrow, shortly after dawn, but hadn't.

Leaving the cats under the bed, which is where all cats live for a week after emigration, our friend and his son drove down to the village to buy bread and so on. On their way back they passed the plumber, his task completed, on the road, to find when they got home that someone had broken a single pane of glass in the french window at the back, entered and ransacked the house from top to bottom, working to too tight a schedule, however, to perform the usual clean sweep. Nothing, in fact, seemed to be missing, but our friend said he was glad he had the price of the new car he intends to buy in his pocket, in cash, rather than in the top right-hand drawer, where he'd nearly left it. The plumber, a very nice young man, worked out that the malefactors might have had four minutes, between his departure and the return of our friend, to do the job.

The result of all this is that it now takes us twenty-five minutes to leave the house, which is the time necessary to close and lock two pairs of shutters upstairs, three pairs downstairs, one pair on my study and the garage doors, which has to have a wooden bar put through the handle on the inside, because the lock's not too good, and this if we're only going across the road for a quick drink. If we're going out for lunch we lock the front gate as well, and that takes a good ten minutes because the lock is large and heavy and rusty for lack of use, but not for much longer.

It might seem ungenerous but I can't wait for the villains to conclude their holiday and to return to their normal pursuits, i.e.: gang murder, drug smuggling, arson and the protection racket. I mean, before we lose the key to our fortified home and have to go back to England and live in Rutlandshire.

Of the essence

Sacred blue, didn't the whole of France go raving mad.

You'd think the Bastille had been taken all over again and they'd found Marie Antoinette still eating cake inside it. One could almost suppose that Napoleon had returned from Elba for the second time, won the battle of Waterloo and gone on to beat the tripes out of Moscow. It was conceivably possible that the French had dug a Channel Tunnel all on their very own and come up somewhere near Bond Street. Jubilation, wonderment, starry-eyed dancing in the streets, with le whiskey à go-go. Yet under all this hysterical excitement a profound, logical, personal belief that this inconceivable miracle hadn't really happened.

What they'd done was to put the clocks on another hour, into something called 'Summer Time', without explosions, injury to passers-by or the bottom falling out of the Seine.

Impossible, unbelievable, but true. An unforgettable, glorious victory for *La Belle France*.

Down here in Provence the pages of *Nice*

Matin, our local newspaper, almost smouldered with the incredible news. On the very front page an immense headline reading:

THIS EVENING AT MIDNIGHT IT WILL BE ONE O'CLOCK IN THE MORNING.

An insupportable allegation, but to prove the truth of it a photograph of a small boy with his index finger on the minute hand of a clock showing the time to be six minutes to 1 a.m., and right beside it a much bigger clock – a really serious, proper French clock – indicating six minutes to midnight.

There was a lot of talk about this. Many of the older women in the village maintained that it was cruel to have so young a child up so late at night fiddling with two clocks – why two, by example? – doing something to the smaller one for reasons that no one could possibly understand.

An even older, agricultural friend of mine, on his way to his vineyard at his unalterable time of 7 a.m., told me that his son had told him that it was really 8 a.m., or so the Government had said. He proposed, he announced stoutly, to work for an extra hour that evening, seeing that the Government had also madly decreed that this would be the shortest Sunday in the year. This firm action on his part, he swore, would put the time back to what it had been before, and would therein remain until the day of his death.

On page twenty *Nice Matin* took on this

conservative attitude with outstanding courage, and several thousand words, but betraying, certainly, their own private doubts about the reality of the device. Their explanation began: 'This evening, at midnight, time is going to make a pirouette. The watches will not believe their hands, the clocks mad and hurried will gain 60 minutes on the legal time.'

Absolutely breathless stuff, when all they have to do is to shove the damn things on an hour, like the British have been doing for years without even thinking about it.

Nice Matin tries to calm itself. 'Concretely,' it goes on, 'many French people will pose to themselves tomorrow morning the fairly silly question: "What time is it?" '

At this point my patience began to crack. For God's sake, if you've put your watch on an hour, like we've been told to do already about twenty-seven times, if you think it's seven o'clock in the morning it is, in a kind of way, but it's really an hour later, sort of.

Realizing that I, too, was beginning to blunder about in a morass of the obvious, I skipped several feet of type and suddenly slammed head-on into a brick wall, with my mind – and watch – stopped dead. *Nice Matin* announces: 'In the space of a second you will have gained in effect one hour. And therefore no one can ask you what you were doing, this Sunday, during midnight and 1 o'clock in the morning.'

Look, you can't stop living just because the clock's been put on. You haven't just disappeared. You must be breathing or reading or – or anything. I see that I am faced with philosophic reflection, or metaphysical messing about and to hell with it.

The whole trouble about this new French summer time is that they used to have it in 1916 and they gave it up because it was silly or not French, in essence. Then France was occupied during World War II by the Germans, who imposed Berlin time on them, an hour ahead in winter and two hours ahead in summer. When the Germans retired in 1945 the French went back to real, unmuckable French time, and didn't want to hear any more about it, until now, when we're an hour ahead.

Next morning, in a more *tranquille* state of mind, I opened the *Daily Telegraph*, who told me, on Page One, that the French had put their clocks *back* an hour, and I began screaming at the wall.

Red Baron grounded

When *la Baronne* – a promotion for Madame the reason for which will be revealed, excitingly, later on – when *la Baronne* said that she was going 'for a couple of hours flying around with Pete in a little two-seater plane' she quadrupled this madness by suggesting that I should go in her place, adding, 'It would give you something interesting to do.'

I was on to this sketchily veiled insult in a flash. 'You suggest that thus far, this year, all my activities have been of an uninteresting nature?'

'Well,' she said, side-stepping this shaft, 'Pete's got to go anyway, to get in some hours before the end of the month, to keep his licence. It would surely give you—'

'—something to write about. Thank you,' I said, 'but I never fly with people I know. You see, I'd be so sorry for them being so sorry for me just before we – struck.' I chose the amplification as though with a pair of eyebrow tweezers. 'That is – if anything – happened.'

'You know perfectly well that Pete is an absolutely first-class pilot.'

'Ah, but what about the others? What about a giant Jumbo snoring out of Nice Airport and running you down because he's in a hurry to get to New York? In any case, in my current state of agility it would take me an hour to get into a two-seater aeroplane, and twice as long to get out, probably in the sea.'

La Baronne went off with Pete. I countered this move by giving a small, informal lunch party – informal in the sense that Peter and Philip provided the food from their restaurant in Tourettes, with the lovely Nola to serve it, while I kept a sharp eye on the sky.

They came over round about one o'clock, making two complete circuits above us at about eight hundred feet. We waved, performing at the same time a facsimile of an African tribal dance – a curious, if routine, reaction to friends passing above in small aeroplanes. We resumed lunch as they disappeard in a southerly direction. *La Baronne* came back, by land, a couple of hours later with reports of a most enjoyable flight, marred only by a certain difficulty in finding her own house from the air. They had, it seemed, made quite a long search in the vicinity, before finding us dancing for them.

Next morning, Pete rang up with strange news. The police had called upon him, with a number of polite but obviously searching questions.

They wanted to know if he had been flying

yesterday, and if so from where? Pete said he had indeed been flying, out of Cannes-Mandelieu, the base for nearly all civil aircraft in these parts.

And where had he flown to?

Pete said that he'd gone over Cannes and then over the islands and subsequently turned inland.

In which direction?

At this point, apparently, Pete began to crack a bit. He asked him to tell him, plainly, if they believed he had infringed any flying regulations and if so, which one? Or ones?

The police said that nothing of that kind had happened. On the other hand, he had flown for a considerable period in the neighbourhood of the Poniatowsky Château. Why?

Everything dropped into place. Prince Poniatowsky is the father of Michel Poniatowsky, former Minister for the Interior, in France. He has a house on his father's estate, so the whole place is guarded by a heavy armament by day and by night. Unknown visitors, by land or by air, are not welcome.

Pete, much relieved, explained that his guest, *la Baronne* Glenavy, had merely been looking for her own house, from the air, and that it was just down the road from the Château. Furthermore, *la Baronne* – and her husband, *le Baron* – had been friends of the Prince and Princess Poniatowsky for quite some time, and wished them no harm of any kind.

The police appeared to be satisfied and went away. For myself, in the guise of *le Baron* Glenavy, I found it mildly gratifying to have got, at long last, at least a small toe-hold in on the act.

Next day, a police van stopped outside our house and then went round the back to interview our neighbour. After they'd gone André told us they'd wanted to know our name. 'But you've got so many names,' André said, 'I don't know any of them. I told them the *M'sieu* was at home, and they'd better ask *him*.'

They didn't. They just went away.

A proper swizz. With all these private planes and police and Princes and Ministers flying around it's not very kind to leave the Red Baron standing there uselesly in the wings, with a squashy mushroom omelette all over his face.

Strapped in sparadrap

Many newspapers at holiday time try to help their readers by casting a heavy medical cloud over their coming holidays, foreseeing gashings, hackings, breakages and poisonings that would almost certainly not have happened if they'd stayed at home, in bed, with room service, instead of setting out for Djerba, Colwyn Bay or anywhere in the world that is more than ten miles away from where they live.

Our local French newspaper is particularly juicy in their remedies for the blood-stained shambles that is so surely on its way, seeing that as from this morning onwards two and a half million French families will be trying to make their way north at exactly the same time as precisely the same number will be struggling south, neither army adhering too rigidly to their own side of the road.

This is not to say that they propose medication for the results of multiple car crashes at ninety mph, in that, in advance, it is difficult to estimate what treatment will be required. They are more concerned with irritants like temporary immobilization, fever, sprains, bee stings, etc. which, in addition to prostrating the victim, will *par ricochet*, or in a roundabout way, affect the whole of the rest of the family – a shrewd assessment of the dangers involved.

I was particularly taken by a piece about the travelling chemist's shop and its tools – *la panoplie* – that the far-sighted traveller will take with him in the interests of his own survival and, if anything is left over, for the assuagement of similar ills afflicting his companions.

In the space of about five minutes, in fact,

I became an expert on the things that can happen to French people in their own language, a knowledge denied to me, through idleness, before. Take, for instance, *le spara-drap* – surely a skin infection approaching leprosy in a more serious case. But a *spara-drap* is only a piece of sticking plaster! If you get an infection of the *amygdales* you must almost certainly be done for, but it's only tonsillitis. *Velpeau*, sounding fatal, is a crepe bandage, whilst *le garrot*, far from being a length of choking wire, is only a tourniquet, in case you rupture a vein or get bitten by a viper.

But how to employ all this new and exceedingly helpful information? How can I get next to an English family, in their own car, in urgent need of medical advice? I'm certainly not going to go down to the teeming beaches, Florence Nightingaleing, and come back, personally, with an agonizing attack of *spara-drap*. Better let them come to me. Perhaps they wandered up this way, having got lost, and suddenly a veritable geyser of steam bursts from their labouring engine outside our very gate. Easy to see how that could happen. At the last stop for petrol the *garagiste* offered to look at their *niveaux*. In the belief that he was trying to sell them a whole new set of shock absorbers they sped away, with an engine empty of both oil and water, ingredients which he was offering to check.

Well, anyway, there they are outside the gate, in a cloud of steam, a man, his wife, two children and a mother-in-law, looking in pretty poor shape. I mend their car with water and oil and then give my patients a cursory examination. The husband looks a bit bulgy round the neck. I ask him, 'How are your *amygdales?*'

He and his wife exchange a startled look.

'In case,' I explain, 'you have to see a doctor I'm giving you this technical stuff in French.' I give a comfortable doctor's chuckle. 'I mean, if he's had his *amygdales* out we don't want to see him treated with the *garrot.*'

Both of them clutch their necks in sudden fear.

'That child in the back there,' I tell them, 'the fat one, looks as if she could do with a greasy net impregnated with balsam around her upper arm. Nasty scratch. Just ask the doctor for a *tulle gras imbibée* with a *baume spécial.* It'll do the trick in a trice.'

The driver, unfairly, seems to be about to lose his temper. 'Look, here, sir,' he says, 'what's all this damn nonsense about? We're all perfectly well.'

Le Docteur Combel replies promptly, 'That's what you think. If that's your mother-in-law in the back and she hasn't had it already I'd give her a dose of alcohol at 90°. Just sprinkle it on some *coton hydrophile* – cottonwool to the layman – and dab it that *plaie* on her hooter. You'd call it a boil.' I break off, dramatically. 'Oh dear, oh dear,' is my exclamation. 'That other child is drenched in mercurochrome. If you put it on more than once you've gone and let the wolf loose in the sheepfold. Another French medical term. *Enferme le loup dans la bergerie.* Sealing in the microbes. You might as well strap her up in *sparadr—*'

I'm interrupted by the car roaring away – probably to a doctor who's in for more trouble than he's ever known.

Pussy paradise

The problem is what to do with Spotty and Dotty before we leave for London.

Spotty and Dotty are the black and white, semi-wild kittens who were lopped by the vet and as a result fell so deeply in love with both of us that they lean against us in a swooning ecstasy of devotion and fall down when we move away. They appear to believe that their operations saved them from death or, at the very least, some crippling disease, and are now intent – every waking moment of the day – in showing their gratitude and – all night long – leaping about on the bed to defend us against whatever demons may be abroad, during the dangerous hours of darkness.

It would be unkind to leave them to fend for themselves, in spite of the fact that several neighbours are prepared to come in and cook them three or four hot meals a day. They want us there to lean against and – in any case – the hunting season is in full blast around here so that anything that moves, probably including worms, is exterminated with instant dispatch. Neither Spot nor Dot look like pheasants, hares or wild boar, but if a worm, putting its head up for a brief moment, can get both barrels between the eyes, why not them?

But where to find temporary lodgings? The French, while very hot on dogs, regard cats as machines for cleaning up mice and other vermin, and feed them – if they feed them at all – on soup and rejected tomatoes.

Nonetheless, we called on a newly opened *pension* for *animaux* in the neighbourhood, and while still half-a-mile away were deafened by the roaring of boxers, the booming of Alsations, the yelping of poodles, the squeaking of Pekingese. A maelstrom of mindless barking and in the middle of it a cage of tottering, elderly cats drinking dusty water from tin bowls. Not at all the kind of thing to which Spo and Do had become accustomed.

Then we heard of another place miles away in the mountains above Fayence, practically in another country, and set out to research it, perhaps foolishly concerned about the future comfort and happiness of Spout and Doubt.

The summer had come back in blazing blue after last week's two days of grey and bitter winter. We drove for miles through pinewoods and bare hills covered with yellow flowers and suddenly, there it was in a narrow lane, a drawing of Pluto on a notice board and the name, 'Pension Bois Fleurie'.

I left the car in the shade of a pine tree and we started to walk through the wood towards a low white house in the distance. A dog barked. A large lady came out of the house. She advanced upon us and, without warning, the whole wood was alive with dogs, leaping and dancing and galloping towards us, and I swear that every single one of them was laughing. There were poodles and terriers and dachshunds and a great dane puppy with three miniature doglets churning away between his enormous legs. They surrounded us, laughing and pushing and tumbling one another over. There must have been thirty or forty of them and not one of them tried to jump up on us, having too much fun among themselves.

The lady introduced herself as Madame Gautier, and then took us on a tour of her flowery wood. Two of the smallest doglets got left behind on their inch-long legs so I gave them a lift on the palm of my hand. The great dane puppy rushed through an ornamental pond and came out the other side with a mouthful of weed. A siamese cat with a poodle friend, conversing in the shade, looked away disdainfully.

It was a truly incredible place. There was a wire enclosure full of ducks, peahens and golden pheasants. A doglet squeaked at a duck through the wire and the duck replied with the friendliest of quacks. A regal white persian cat stalked around his own home – a ladder leading upstairs to his private bedroom – acting the film-star for a group of poodles, having the best of sport in sending him up.

Mme Gautier showed us Spotty and Dotty's holiday home – ladder leading to double bedroom, quite close to the ducks. 'Perhaps,' she said, 'it would interest them, if they have not seen such birds before.'

We went into the office, to make arrangements, followed by a busy group of doglets, dachshunds and poodles who pulled out chairs, found files and made themselves generally useful.

We deliver Spot and Dot this afternoon. Privately, we know that neither of us would mind moving right in there with them.

Paternal triangle

The French Government's warm, paternal care for its millions of potentially wayward motorists got one of its regular upsurges of love a few years ago when it said, as suddenly as ever, that from now on we all had to carry a *dispositif* in our veritable vehicles.

Like many another foreign resident I read about this new law in our local newspaper, in a paragraph of four or five lines submerged in a page otherwise devoted to congenial fetes in old persons' homes, plus photographs of every single inhabitant. Unfortunately, this Draconian edict's force was futher camouflaged from me by the fact that I'd never seen the word *dispositif* before, much less having heard it used in polite conversation. A hurried scuffle through the dictionary left me out on a notably slender limb, seeing that *dispositif* means 'an apparatus, device, contrivance or appliance' – stuff with which every motor-car known to man must be filled to the brim, already. Seeing that savage fines were promised for not having a *dispositif* I arranged an urgent meeting with our garage proprietor, from whom I learnt to my astonishment that a

126

dispositif was a large, red plastic collapsible triangle, normally carried in a white plastic tube, which had to be erected and left one hundred yards behind any vehicle that might break down on a public thoroughfare. He happened, by sheer chance, to have this very contrivance in stock and let me have one at the cost of £8.

Like all new laws this one got rapidly bent. Many a French motorist, bowling along a country lane without a *dispositif*, saw one carefully erected by the side of the road in front of him, stopped, shoved the whole contraption into the boot of his car, and sped on past the previous owner, struggling with a puncture and oblivious, for the moment, to the nefarious goings-on that had taken place round the corner behind him. Further, even filthier, cases were reported. Law-abiding motorists, having mended their punctures, walked back to reclaim their *dispositif*, only to find it had gone and, upon running back to their car, that it had gone too, they having lamentably left the ignition key in their appliance.

After that, however, things went well with my motoring. I had no punctures or other breakdowns and by keeping the *dispositif* locked in the boot I still had it a year later. And then came this next blow, landed by a paternal government, an uppercut picked straight up off the floor. It seemed, *per pro* yet another inconspicuous newspaper paragraph, that as from February the first in this current year, any motor-car in France exuding more than four and a half per cent carbon monoxide from its exhaust pipe would incur a fine of ten quid, after scientific testing by police patrols covering every inch of the countryside. Nor was this all. A second offence, committed by the same vehicle, would win a fine of £20. And this only chicken-feed, in view of the fact that a third offence would be rewarded with *eight days – and nights – in prison.*

I slid back to our garage as unobtrusively as a snake, with the car at fifteen mph, scarcely breathing out at all, and there was the proprietor, ever far-sighted, with a brand-new sample of the very same exhaust-sniffing machine employed by the police and probably stuffing every prison in France.

We coupled up the exhaust-sniffer, revved her up and got seven and a half per cent carbon monoxide pollution! Probably the guillotine, rather than a mere eight-day stretch.

He began, without apparent optimism, to tighten and slacken those mysterious little screws that do so much, or so little, for the modern carburettor. Our pollution rose to nine per cent. Putting in motion the plan he'd almost certainly had in mind already, he suggested I leave the car with him until he cured the fault. 'With a brand-new engine?' I said, in jest. 'One never knows,' he replied, rather more seriously.

I passed the next three days as pleasantly as possible in frightening the life out of all the friends who hadn't, as yet, heard about the new law, sending them scurrying off to their own garages in search of the fatal test, before they began packing pyjamas and toiletries for prison.

When I got my own car back I also got a *Carte Blanche*, confirming only a three per cent pollution, valuable for 10,000 kilometres or a year. It was like receiving the *Légion d'Honneur*, but as yet without the bill. It also said that, 'This is in your own interests – and in the interests of everyone else'.

It will be interesting to see how long it takes everyone else to bend this one, probably substituting my immaculate engine for their own and removing at the same time my unused *dispositif*.

Things tend to go like that under a truly paternal government.

Rummed all round

This pretty, vivacious French lady comes flying in through the gate, silk scarves fluttering, bangles all a-jangle, and before we have time to put up any defence at all she jams us into the position of driving her to Cannes the following evening – husband away, all alone, no car, etc. – so that she can buy us dinner in a restaurant which she describes as being 'not sad, like all the others'. She dances away down the road towards her own house before, as I have said, we can intrude a single 'But—' or an 'Unfortunately—', and we have plenty of them in store for just a situation as this.

By an unlucky chance we have just given two lunch parties in a row, both of which turned – without perceptible interval – into dinner parties, so that the very last thing we wish to do is to find ourselves in a not sad restaurant the very next night, laughing like hyenas, in French. And particularly, as the very last thing, far beyond the very last thing, in Cannes, which is half an hour away and is, therefore, absolutely unvisitable by either of us after dark.

However, two very good things happen the following morning. Madame, working away at it like a beaver, has managed to find herself a superb sore throat and, furthermore, an equal blessing, it is belting rain, with the clear intention of continuing to do so for the next three weeks.

It is with a song in my heart, under my golf umbrella, with mud up to my sock clocks, that I prance up the drive to the French lady's house, to tell her that I am desolated but we cannot dine with her in Cannes tonight. This lady, with – temporarily

– no husband and no car, has gone out. I don't know how she's got out, in this torrent, but got out she has, not – perhaps – having got back the previous night.

I have had to pay this abortive visit in person because the lady, of course, has no telephone, so that having dried myself as best I can I sit down to write her a short note, to be shot into her letter-box by hand, upon completion.

I begin, '*Chere Jacqueline*—' and absolutely upon that instant I remember that while I can speak French, in a saw-toothed way, I am entirely unable to write it. Has, for instance, *chere* got an acute accent on the first *e*? If I don't insert the acute accent does it mean something else altogether, like instead of 'Dear Jacqueline—' am I writing, 'Expensive Jacqueline'?

Out with the dictionary and, by gum, I'm right. *Cher* hasn't got one, but *chère* has. A narrow escape. I'm off, then. '*Chère Jacqueline – si ça vous derange pas*—'

I want to say, 'If it doesn't inconvenience you' but it looks as if I've said, 'If that doesn't drive you out of your mind.'

It's *derange* that looks wrong. Too much like the onset of homicidal mania. Perhaps *it* has an acute accent and – by gum again – it has.

'*Chère Jacqueline – si ça vous dérange pas*—' Much better, much Frenchier. '*—je voudrais bien changer la nuit de notre rendez-vous a Vendredi*—'

131

I would wish well to change the night of our assignation to Friday. Pretty rough stuff and even at that it seems to be missing something. Out with the red-hot dictionary again and I find to my total amazement that *notre* means 'our', but if you glue a circumflex on to the 'o' it means 'ours'. The which I was about to do. 'Ours assignation—' And surely there is something wrong with '*a Vendredi*'? Has Friday. Of course! The damn thing's got a grave accent '—*à Vendredi*'. To think I missed by a hairsbreadth telling expensive Jacqueline that ours assignation has Friday! The poor woman wouldn't have known which way to turn.

On then, encouraged, to the pith of the communication. '*La pauvre Vivienne est tellement enrhumée—*' It can't be.

The impoverished Vivienne is muchly rummed. My wife, dressed in rags, is stiff with Bacardi and a slice of lemon.

Dictionary. A winner! '*Être enrhumé* – to have a cold.' But I note, with a shudder, that the perfectly commonplace word *être* has a circumflex on the first *e* – a thing I'd never known before, or hadn't noticed. Resolve to keep clear of *that*.

Now, to round it all off. '*Et voila – quel temps!*' And there it is – what time!

But that has to be right because that's what everyone says when it's raining. *Except* that the French, according to the dictionary, say '*Voilà*' with *un accent grave* on the *à*. The awkward foreign swine.

132

I am about to push this back-breaking work through Jacqueline's letter-box when she opens the door herself. In a barely audible croak she says she doesn't want to derange me, but she is muchly rummed – 'Et voilà,' she cries, 'le temps!'

If only she'd said even half of that before I got going . . .

Twice times Eugene

The telephone (French) rings, not with the almost chirpy little double tring-tring of the British instrument but in a series of widely spaced metallic belches, sonorous and doom-laden, that seems to announce, '*Me . . . Me . . . Me . . .*'

I pick up the receiver and, in case the party of the first part is French, I say, '*Allo – oui?*', but knowing at the same time it's an even-money shot that it's going to be someone saying, 'Oh, hello, darling – that's only you, is it – *she's* not there?'

But on this occasion it is, indeed, French and a woman, at that, with one of those French female voices with much of the resonance of a large file biting into corrugated iron.

My '*Allo – oui?*' is greeted with an exceed-ingly peremptory, '*Allo*'. Then a note of doubt seems to intrude itself. Without being absolutely certain about it she thinks I might be a man and, if that be the case, what then is going on? She says, '*Madame Frantic Nelly n'est pas là?*' It is abundantly clear that she thinks Frantic Nelly is standing beside me, holding her nose between finger and thumb and pulling an imaginary chain.

I know I haven't got her friend's (?) name right, but in this French-Italian area it's quite easy for a woman to be called some-thing quite like Frantic Nelly. I tell her, matching her own rising fury, that not only is Madame Frantic Nelly not here but she's never even been here, because here she has never lived.

I can see the party of the first part reeling back from her receiver as though I had expelled a blast of fetid air straight into her lug. She lies back on the ropes for a moment and then springs back into the fight with a ramrod straight left.

'*C'est pas possible!*'

I've almost worn out the canvas in this particular ring in countless brutal battles owing to the fact that no French person will ever believe they have dialled a wrong num-ber. They have dialled a number – any number – but this must be the right one. Furthermore, of all the people in the world that might have answered the call there can be only one who has done so: i.e. the person they are looking for.

I let her have a crunching right cross. 'I regret, Madame, but you have dialled the wrong number.'

We really begin to mix it. She wants to know what our number is. I counter by asking her what number she is calling. In a scream she gives me our number. I cover up into the defensive ploy of Frantic Nelly never having been here or ever likely to get in and while she's yelling about all that being impossible I give her a really savage clout in the solar plexus. 'Ring Directory Enquiries and leave me in tranquility – goodbye.' Before I can put down the phone she slips in a rattle of kidney punches based upon, 'Clod, beast, imbecile, *English*—'. But I'm not bothered. Directory Enquiries, if she's mad enough to ring them, are going to do my work for me, pounding her into small lumps in a single round.

If you ring Directory Enquiries they begin talking very quickly and angrily before you can get in more than three words, particularly if the three words indicate that you're looking for the number of a restaurant the name and locality of which you know perfectly well but which cannot be found in the telephone book.

Directory Enquiries, bellowing away, want to know if it's a bar, a restaurant, a snack-bar, a pizzeria, a brasserie or, by sheer clumsy chance, does the subscriber happen to know the proprietor's name? In any case, whatever the subscriber is looking for, will he spell it out, at once, letter by letter?

Anatole. Berthe. Célestin. Kléber. Quintal. Thérèse. Ursule. Xavier. Irma. Zoé . . . Not on your life.

I actually know a man who once rang Enquiries about a number in Los Angeles and before he could begin to spell anything Enquiries did it for him. 'Louis Oscar Suzanne Eugène Nicholas Gaston Eugène Louis deux fois Eugène.' *L'os en gelée.* Or a jellied bone.

The French, whose highly individual spirit I dearly love, really only like talking to one another face to face and both, for hours on end, at the same time. It's the awkward mechanism of the telephone that gets in their way and infuriates them, the soulless barrier between the always invigorating personal fusion or clash.

Still, I'm always glad to get a call from London, with the dove-like voice of the secretary apologizing every minute for keeping me waiting because the man who's trying to call *me* has just left his office and cannot be found.

At least, however impatient I may get, she's not going to accuse me of being English.

All Over the Place

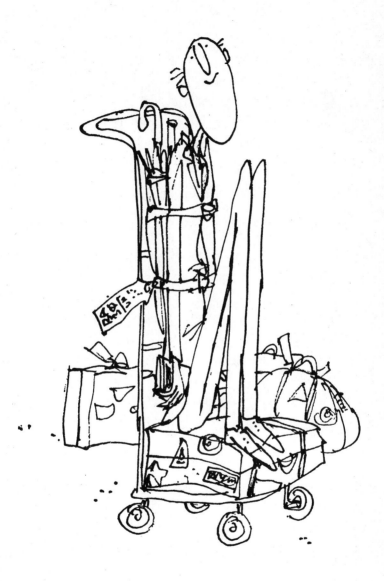

East is *West*

Under normal conditions of travel those moving walkways they have at airports are stationary, with three men – almost out of sight – effecting repairs to the machinery at the other end.

That is to say one man beats the machinery with a sledgehammer while the other two stand by with crowbars so that if the moving walkway actually begins to move again they can stop it by jamming their crowbars into its vitals.

At London Airport the other morning, however, the walkways in Terminal Three were in motion, probably for the reason that the hammer and crowbar executives were having a tea-break or were on strike, so that my wife and I were able to cover the four miles separating the Departure Lounge from Gate 22 without effort. It was quite pleasant leaning against the moving banister watching elderly passengers laden with plastic bags and bulging hold-alls doing it the hard way, legging it along beside us on foot, either because they didn't know about the walkway or knew it only too well – with its habit of suddenly stopping and flinging everyone to the ground, if not making a real job of it by going into reverse.

The preliminaries to flying, the actual getting into the aircraft, were normal, being very similar to entanglement, abroad, with British soccer fans celebrating either victory or defeat, but once we had taken our seats amid Thai International's Royal Orchid Service it was as though we had been dropped into a mixed and singularly luxurious harem.

I would be the very last one, of course, to attempt to cast a slur upon European female attendants in aeroplanes, but would it be going too far to suggest that their physical proportions and spiritual characteristics tend not altogether to fit them for all the exigencies of the job?

We all know, for instance, the lovely blonde, Doreen, trim as a new pin, who greets us so courteously at the door of the aeroplane. No item of Doreen, be it in her uniform or person, is out of place.

'Good morning, sir,' says Doreen, and we wonder, in theory, what she is doing tonight.

This is Doreen at her very best. This is Doreen, standing upright, at rest, with her cap on. This is Doreen before the job begins to get at her. The ideal Doreen, as it were, and all we scientific hostess-watchers know that it's not going to last.

Doreen's scrambler arrives almost at once – a flustered, elderly woman with two handbags, one inside the other and both full. She also carries a tartan overnight bag with a broken zipper and another plastic one filled, as far as one can make out, with mixed groceries, in tins.

She gets about half of this load into the luggage rack before Doreen spots her and by the time Doreen gets it off the luggage rack and under the elderly woman's seat several disagreeable things have happened to Doreen.

At the back, her shirt has come away from the top of her skirt, and protrudes. Her cap has been nudged forward over her eyes, and is crooked. Also, her neck is getting hot and changing colour and the previously piled up hair is coming, slightly, down. And all this before the fat man in Row F tips his feed bowl into his lap and the violent child in Row C suddenly cants his seat backwards and bangs a bottle of stout straight into the face of the man in Row D, who has been leaning forward the better to get it down.

Soon, someone will stand on Doreen's foot, someone else with a penetrating laugh will ask her what she's doing tonight, nudging the missus at the same time, so that long before we come in to land Doreen is wishing she had a quiet and dignified job on the buses, or in a butcher's shop.

Doreen does not have the advantages of Miss Suparb. Where Doreen is large and hot Miss Suparb is tiny and for ever cool. Where Doreen's temper verges upon the uncertain adversity seems to be a lovely joke to Miss Suparb.

It was Miss Suparb who met us at the door of the harem that was going to whip us to Bangkok, 5,930 miles away.

At first, when she saw us, I thought she had burst into tears. She placed her fragile ivory palms together and into them buried her lovely face, appalled – I considered – by my monstrous and ungainly Irish size. But this is only the Thai national greeting and a moment later the whole plane was filled with her delighted smile.

Through the long day and the night that came so quickly we fell more and more in love with the Thai smile. At one moment they are the regulation inscrutable Oriental. At the next this smile flashes out and you'd really think you were back in the Garden of Eden, before Eve started all the aggro.

You need a smile like this to ease your conscience as you fly, with champagne and caviar, across the tormented world. Below you, the Russians are leaning on Eastern Europe, the Turks are leaning on the Greeks, the Shah of Persia on Denis Healey and India is starving from Delhi to Calcutta. But there is Miss Suparb, noiselessly flitting up and down with hot towels and cold drinks, and for the whole twelve hours she remains, in her pink silk jacket and long lime-green skirt, as unchangingly beautiful as a jewel, but a jewel illuminated as regularly as a lighthouse by this incredible, flashing smile.

The Turkish night came on in the middle of the English afternoon. It was pitch dark as we landed to refuel at Teheran. It was 11 p.m. in London when a blood-red dawn came up over Burma and Miss Suparb laid breakfast before us without a sound.

Disorientated, jet-lagged and covered with cigarette ash we stepped out into the steamy, molten air of Bangkok, to be garlanded with orchids, jasmine and frangi-pani by another tiny Thai beauty, with the same entirely dazzling smile. Behind us tripped Miss Suparb, with her suitcase, going home, as fresh as the moment when she left London.

If we'd had Doreen along the three of us could have shared the same stretcher to the waiting car.

There is indeed something infinitely mysterious about the Far East.

Before taking off from London we had scarcely time to find that we were sitting on our glasses and on the ends of one another's seat belts before a courteous voice behind us said, 'Do let me give you a glass of champagne later on – it's free.'

I turned and there was the very individual who had borrowed a fiver off me at Leopardstown race course round about 1934, with the promise of a fifty per cent share in an investment on an animal starting at the discouraging price of 22/1. It won by four lengths, suggesting that some arrangement had been made before the off, but it was no quicker than my co-punter whom I was not to see again until this very moment, sitting immediately behind us and bound, like ourselves, for Bangkok, probably at someone else's expense, including mine, if one took the long view.

From the airport we went to the Trocadero Hotel, where we had borrowed an appartment from a man we'd never met, but Dirk Bogarde was smiling at us from above the bed. Not Dirk in person but Dirk on a poster for *Death in Venice*. He lives ten minutes away from us in the South of France and we'd had lunch with him the day before we left for the mysterious and congested East.

From Bangkok we went to Hong Kong, to the luxury of the Mandarin Hotel and a suite overlooking the harbour. The entirely delightful manager, Peter Stafford, now moved on, asked us to lunch in his Man Wah Restaurant. There were three other guests. Madame looked at one of them. 'Hello,' she said, 'you're Don Ashton. We used to work together in Shepperton Film Studios.' It then turned out, amid a cascade of other revelations, that Don Ashton had designed the sets for *Oh What A Lovely War*, directed by Richard Attenborough. And Dickie has a house in the South of France immediately beside Mr Bogarde's.

During the course of Old Home Week in

the Man Wah the third guest, in addition to Mr and Mrs Ashton, scarcely spoke, mostly because he couldn't find a crevice into which to insert a word. He was an Australian surgeon, obviously out of touch with London showbusiness – until he did speak. 'I suppose,' he said, 'you know an English film director called Jack Lee.'

'Jack!' we cried. 'Brother of Laurie Lee, living in Sydney.'

'That's him,' said the third guest. 'I took out his prostate last week.'

From Hong Kong we went to Singapore, to that magical institution Raffles Hotel. A huge and heavily moustached American lurched up to the bar, almost knocking the man beside us off his stool, and lurched away again, bent upon some private business of his own. The man beside us smiled. 'Extraordinary,' he said, in a cultured English voice, 'for a moment I could have sworn he was—'

Madame said, 'Cracker Harris.'

The man said, 'You don't know Cracker – from Maidenhead!'

Madame said, 'I thought it was him, too.'

'But then,' the man said, 'you must know Mary – and Trevor – and Pete.'

Madame said, 'I shared a flat with Mary in London during the war and begged her time after time not to ditch Trevor for that rat Pete.'

They had a splendid bash at the Mary-Trevor-Rat Pete theme and then the man said,

'Look, have dinner with me. The fact is, I've been stood up. I come down here quite often for a spot of monkey business, leaving the wife in Kuala Lumpur. Actually, she's Mary's daughter.'

'She is also,' Madame said, 'my god-child.'

From Singapore we went back to Bangkok, and in Bangkok we went out to look at the Crocodile Farm.

The man beside me with a movie camera was taking pictures of the crocodile controller hoisting a crocodile on to his back. He stopped when he saw that the crocodile wasn't going to make an early lunch, turned to me and said, 'Good morning, Mr Campbell. Do you remember giving me your *Sunday Times* column at Nice Airport, about three weeks ago?'

During the chronic French postal strikes I used to take my column down to the airport every Wednesday, neatly stamped and addressed, give it so someone who was going to London on the British Airways flight, and here was one of those Mr Someones standing beside me in the Crocodile Farm.

Rudyard Kipling said that East was East and West was West and what I say is that the Twain are stuck together, like the ghosts in a metaphorical sense, of Noël Coward and Willy Maugham.

At one moment in Willy Maugham's bed in Raffles Hotel, Singapore – at the next in Noël Coward's Chinese boudoir in the Oriental Hotel, Bangkok!

Difficult, now, to get closer to the Masters than that, but even this remote connection seemed to go to my head.

We were scarcely into Willy's suite in Raffles before I was on the phone to room service, requesting tomato juice, Worcester sauce, fresh limes and so on, making no mention, of course, of the fact that we were already supplied with duty-free vodka – the effect of which is more shattering than ever in the Far East, where it retails at £8 a bottle.

House boy come chop-chop – with a two-litre flagon of tomato juice, which he could scarcely carry. 'You want six like this?' he enquired. I had, in fact, ordered six *tins*, expecting them to be of European size. 'You fill swimming-pool?' he asked with Chinese inscrutability, which manifests itself in the form of wild, delighted laughter.

I straightened the matter out, giving him either a king's ransom or fourpence in Singapore dollars, and looked out into the Palm Court with Willy's eyes.

Unlike its counterpart in, say, Eastbourne, Raffles' Palm Court is open to the steamy equatorial skies, with sixty-foot palm trees soaring from the grass. Having a look for Willy I was distressed on his behalf to see that the pool was filled with children and its edges lined with collapsible prams. Rather a far cry from the Colonel's wife being languid in a one-piece bathing-suit, beneath the burning eyes of Captain Dashwood, but then the pool was put in in 1970 and Willy was last there in 1959, so that he would have been spared the happy little nippers.

In the hotel itself it was much more Maughamy. The billiard table is still there under which the tiger was shot by the head-master of the neighbouring school. The Long Bar is much shorter than it was, but about to be restored to its former glories, and fairly sinister figures still lurk about in safari jackets, drinking gin slings. In a city, burst-ing with forty-five-storey American-style hotels Raffles remains uniquely itself, even presenting us, on cue, with Adultery. Rangy Australian lady, jet-black hair, laden with jewels, buying champagne (£35 per bot.) for plump and bearded German boy in a tight silk suit, while Theresa Khoo at the piano, getting mixed up with Noël, played *Some Day I'll Find You*. Hard drinking American, the remnants of Errol Flynn, in the company of a beautiful Chinese girl, waiting to kill him, and/or go home.

We had to leave them to it and fly off to the Noël Coward Suite in the Oriental. Two photographs of the Master in the sitting-room and below us the garden and the swiftly flowing vegetable soup of the Chaophraya, the River of Kings. Two Chinese fourposters, in the green and gold boudoir, but no plaque to indicate in which of them the Master had laid his sweet head.

Next morning, on the lawn, six impossibly

beautiful Thai girls in national costume performed a stately dance, to the sound of flutes
and drums. At the end of it they posed in one
of the figures of the dance, double-jointed
fingers protruding in every direction. After
quite a long time a strange thing happened.
From the shade of the surrounding trees
there burst a horde of foreigners, looking
lumpish and hot in their western clothes,
each and every one of them armed with a
camera. They fought and scrambled and fell
over one another, taking happy snaps of the
girls. Beside me, I felt the Master humming
in that light tenor voice;

> *In Bangkok*,
> At twelve o'clock,
> *They foam at the mouth and run*,
> *But mad dogs and Englishmen*
> *Go out in the midday sun.*

Standing there at the window of the Oriental,
despite the thundering engines of the river
boats, the charter tours and the plethora of
Japanese cameras, I felt I was right back
again to the Thirties, to Cavalcade, to all
those Cochran revues, to *Mad Dogs and
Englishmen* and all the rest of the Master's
brittle and brilliant music.

Strange, the potency of luxurious hotels,
though I'm sure the Master probably stayed
most of the time in the security of his.

★

Bangkok itself comes out swinging like a Thai boxer, using fists, feet, elbows and knees in an all-out assault that seems to come from every direction simultaneously, culminating in a paralysing buffet right up the jumper at the very moment when the sweating *farahng* thinks the worst must surely be over.

'*Farahng*' is the Thai word for a foreigner, but we're certainly not going to go into the Thai language seeing that good morning, good evening, goodnight, hello, goodbye and – probably – give my regards to your father are all represented by '*Sawaht dee*', except if you're a man you say, '*Sawaht dee krahp*' and if you're a woman, if you can still identify your sex, you say, '*Sawaht dee ka*'. And even then if you give it the wrong tone it could in all likelihood mean, 'May I have a new cathode tube for my television set?' At a dinner party I convulsed a delightful Thai princess by trying to pronounce the word '*Mah*' three different ways, giving it three different meanings, but finishing up every time by saying, apparently, 'Horse'. The lady, wiping her lovely dark eyes, said, 'But you can't get out of the stables.'

The first blow that Bangkok delivers – an elbow on top of the head that goes right through to the spine – is the heat. An aristocratic English lady, descending from the plane, is said to have cried, 'It's like stepping into somebody's armpit!' and at that she was toying with words.

In winter the pearl-grey sky sears the eyeballs and the air is simply invisible steam. Then you get into an air-conditioned taxi and you're instantly deep-frozen, like a pork chop.

The taxi tears along a dead-straight, dead-level dual-carriageway, weaving in and out of huge, rusty buses with fifty people inside glued together like over-done rice and suddenly you're up to the hubcaps in water dodging rocks, mountains of gravel and potholes a foot deep. A high tide has pushed the Chaophraya River into the heart of the city, leaving the British Club, where roast beef and Yorkshire pud are on the menu for lunch, isolated in its own lagoon.

Then we're on another dead-straight, dead-level boulevard – the nearest hill is one hundred miles away – turn right without warning and we're in a rutted country lane, lined with tiny houses and tropical trees. We lurch and bump through that and we're on another boulevard again, hemmed in by skyscrapers and luxury hotels, in a herd of thundering, rogue buses, with endlessly blaring horns, motorized tricycles and lorries dripping concrete rubble. The noise and our bitter, air-conditioned cold are beyond belief. We stop outside our hotel, get out of the cab and instantly, from deep-frozen pork chops, we are broiled sweet and sour, with steamed noodles on the side. Up the stairs into the apartment we have borrowed. Air-conditioners like cement mixers whirring in both rooms and in a second we are shivering with cold. On the other side of the road youths with long-handled sledgehammers are demolishing an hotel by hand. The noise from the street is like a tank battle without the gunfire.

There's a knock on the door. A beaming houseboy in the molten heat of the passage outside. I say, '*Sawaht dee krahp.*' He nods delightedly and a moment later comes back with three bottles of mineral water. Obviously, I'll have to watch my language or we'll be knee-deep in it.

But all that was a week – or a month – ago. By now we are either frozen pork or broiled prawn wise old Far Eastern hands. We know enough to dodge the motorcyclists riding on the pavements, blowing their horns. We know enough to drink Mekhong, a deliciously dry rice whiskey distilled last week. We know that 50 Baht is about £1 and can sometimes beat down a taxi-driver from 10 Baht to 7 for a twenty minute ride. We have discovered how to get a sixty per cent reduction on an air-fare to Hong Kong, Kuala Lumpur or Singapore and I can almost stop turning right round to look at the incredibly beautiful girls.

In the midst of the hammering din this is a city devoted with irrepressible enthusiasm to having fun. The lovely, bright faces are always laughing. At midnight the police are there outside the brothel down the street to make sure it closes on time and that the taxis maintain an orderly queue as they wait to take the customers home.

At lunch I was talking to an aristocratic Thai lady with an intimate knowledge of every English magazine from *Encounter* to *Private Eye*.

'But of course,' she said, 'we don't need *Private Eye* here in Bangkok. We are *Private Eye*.'

Following the Pilgrim Fathers

It's just like deer-stalking, except that you don't have to climb the precipitous hills on foot. Indeed, if you do hunt on foot you're liable to be mugged, kidnapped, shot at by the resident deer – reversing the normal discharges – or, if you're lucky, whipped straight back to your hotel by outraged police.

The other resemblance to deer-stalking lies in the fact that the deer – and a lot of stags – are all there, but invisibly camouflaged in their lairs. Also, the quarry is spread out over mile after mile of countryside, so that without an expert White Hunter it's impossible to tell even where to begin to look.

I refer to the stalking of film stars in

Hollywood, not that Hollywood really exists seeing that Hollywood is also kind of Santa Barbara, Malibu Beach, Bel Air, Beverly Hills, Glendale (I think) but certainly also Santa Monica, Palm Springs and Los Angeles.

There is another problem. Mixed in with the stars in their immense bungalows in, say, Bel Air – flood-lit palm trees, guard dogs, electronically operated wrought-iron gates – there are thousands of doctors and lawyers all doing as well as their clients and living in the same magnificent style. Unrewarding, for instance, to gaze at the residence of Rock Hudson, when it turns out that Dr Mervyn Nussbaum has his being there, and I'm glad I mentioned Rock Hudson because we actually had dinner with him, followed by Thanksgiving lunch next day when he wasn't, wisely, in residence.

Our White Hunter was Mark Miller, who is Mr Hudson's business manager. We met Mark when he came to the South of France to see his brother, Philip, who runs this restaurant with another Southern Californian, Peter Launder, in the village of Tourette-sur-Loup. Mark was waiting for us at Los Angeles Airport with the long black Cadillac which is the staple transport around here. A stately process at a petrol-saving, non-polluting thirty mph down boulevards stretching away into infinity, a glimpse of former movie backlots now transformed into millionaire housing estates and suddenly we were in the middle of a real movie set, by courtesy of Twentieth Century Fox. The street scene from *Hello, Dolly* looking far more real than the city itself, leading to the gates of the studio. A nice conceit, when Los Angeles is changing all the time.

Outside the Hudson house was a perfect vintage Ford coupé, one of Mr Hudson's hobbies, and the usual massing of Cadillacs. Inside was Mr Hudson in person, exceedingly tall, slightly silvery in the hair, wearing a handsome lilac shirt and an air of gentlemanly refinement. There was Juliet Mills, sister of Hailey and daughter of Sir John Mills, of London, England, her Czechoslovakian husband; a lady with a very long, surprisingly narrow face; and a friend of Mark's called George Nader, an actor-novelist who can make you laugh without saying anything.

From the terrace the whole of Los Angeles sparkled below us, as Mr Hudson showed me his Jacuzzi pool, a whirling spray device that is all the rage. 'You want to try it?' he asked. I thought he meant fully dressed, which perhaps he did, so I declined. During dinner the narrow-faced lady gave me a highly informed, exceedingly intelligent address about what was wrong with the United States, Great Britain and Europe. Unfortunately, Deborah Kerr, who once visited me in hospital in Dublin, could not be there, as she had had to fly to New York, but we felt it wasn't a bad start to stalking the wily stars.

Next day, Sean Connery and his wife came into the Brown Derby, on Wilshire Boulevard, while we were having lunch. They had just flown in non-stop from Malaga, in Spain. Even Sean's iron frame was blurred by jet-lag. He absorbed a Bloody Mary at a gulp, and solidified.

A couple of nights later we went out to see an old friend from London, Anne Frank, wife of Mel Frank who, having made a lot of money with his picture, *A Touch of Class*, with Glenda Jackson and George Segal, had bought one of the oldest and biggest Spanish haçiendas on Pacific Palisades. It used to belong to the silent star, Lionel Attwill. 'After that,' Anne said, 'some doctors and stuff had it, and now I'm going to do it over.' We ranged through a series of palatial rooms, Anne with expressive gestures breaking out walls and building bow windows. I admired the huge log fire in the living-room. 'It's a fake,' Anne said. 'That's gas. I got to buy the wood ash to make it look good.' It looked just like a huge log fire to me.

That evening Mel was showing a rough-cut of his next movie, *The Duchess and the Dirtwater Fox*. We got into Anne's Cadillac to meet him at the studio. 'I had it nine months,' she said. 'It's already got 9,856 miles on the clock, just shopping. I never even got it out of town.'

We met Mel at a Mexican restaurant called Signor Pico. 'I hope you like tortillas,' he said. We told him we had loved the ones we had had in this very place only yesterday. After the rough-cut, we went to have a drink with the Franks in the Polo Lounge of the Beverly Hills Hotel, where Madame and I were warmly greeted by Antoine, the maître d'hotel. 'You know him?' Mel said. 'Met him last night, right here,' I said. 'He was born in Grasse, ten minutes up the road from us. His sister still works for Fragonard, the perfume people.' Mel said, 'You're getting around.'

Next morning, we met Sir Alec Guinness, buying the London *Times* in the tobacconist shop in the Beverly Wilshire Hotel. 'I am making a picture here,' he said, 'and getting picked up by the police every night. I like walking you see,' he said, voicing the complaint of every visitor to Los Angeles, 'and they keep bringing me home.'

We spent the weekend in Mark's handsome bungalow in Desert Springs, beyond Palm Springs, that nest of multi-millionaires.

I started talking about a triumphantly silly film which I'd seen on television called *The Pride and the Passion*, with Cary Grant as a British naval captain and Frank Sinatra as a Spanish guerilla. 'Directed, to my amazement,' I said, 'by Stanley Cramer,' 'That,' said Mark, 'it was not.' I said, 'I bet you 500,000 dollars it was.' I'd seen the credits three times. Mark made two telephone calls. 'You're right,' he said.

Early the following morning, sitting beside

the heated pool, visibly steaming in the rising desert sun, Mark said, 'Let's ring Peter and Philip in Tourette.' Then he found he'd left the number in his apartment in Los Angeles. 'Never mind,' he said, 'the international exchange will dig it out.'

'In Tourettes?' I said. 'They've never heard of it. I bet you 500,000 dollars it won't work.' The marvellous American telephone system had the number in three minutes. Mark and Philip had an amiable chat for quite some time, at the range of about eight thousand miles, exchanging news and views, information upon the weather and greetings from all present, just as though it were a local call. When it came to an end George sprang out of the house in a voluminous white kaftan, performed a kind of arabesque and leaped into the pool, kaftan and all, arms outspread and feet together. When he surfaced he said, 'I thought I'd just go a little Hollywood for you.'

Later that week, drawn once again into the hub of the Polo Bar in the Beverly Hills, I was almost embraced by a beautiful, youngish woman falling out of the top of her dress who had been kissing everyone else within range. Antoine, from Grasse, smoothly got in the way. She transferred her attentions to a couple of elderly waiters who got jammed in the service door in their retreat.

It's only in California that one realizes the

true meaning of doing your own thing if, that is, you can find yourself, particularly in the limitless wastes of Los Angeles.

Experts who have measured it find, together with all the other cities it has wolfed, that it measures eighty square miles.

Right in the middle of this, on Wilshire Boulevard, is – or was – a tiny red-roofed cottage with pretty bushes outside and beautiful old Rolls Royces within, albeit with white-walled tyres.

One doesn't pass by a phenomenon of this kind. One enters briskly and enquires – no shilly-shallying, please – just what is going on in here.

The cottage, a former restaurant, was in fact a show-room for Rolls of the 1950s, and it was run by a young man with a black moustache called Robert Vallely. (All youthful executives in Los Angeles have exactly the same kind of black moustache, so precisely similar in appearance that one suspects they might be on sale in men's clothing stores.)

Californians are happiest when they are telling strangers, in the most intimate detail and as slowly as possible, as much of the story of their lives as time will allow. Mr Vallely embarked upon his when another young man came in, without a moustache, and said to me, instantly, 'Hello, mate. Last time I saw you you were driving through Vence.' It turned out that he, unmistakably British, had had a restaurant there, a couple of miles away from where we live in the South of France.

I asked him if he was thinking of buying an old Rolls. 'Not me,' he said. 'I'm flogging 'em.' He turned to Mr Vallely. 'I can let you have three Camargues,' he said, 'and as many Silver Shadows as you want.'

Patiently, Mr Vallely began to explain about the prohibitive cost of converting Rolls Royces to comply with American anti-pollution laws. The new arrival interrupted him. 'Mate,' he said, 'whatever you got to do to a Camargue there's bound to be a margin if you're flogging 'em at forty-five thousand quid apiece.'

We left them to it, overwhelmed as ever by the size and style of Californian life, the unimaginable wealth, the limitless distances and the sun that burns day after day throughout the year.

We'd just come back from the weekend in Desert Springs. Two and a half hours' drive in Mark's black Cadillac, air-conditioned, all-electric, George serving hot coffee in the back. At the speed limit of fifty-five mph in a car of that size only the ashtrays could wear out. Palm Springs is covered with emerald-green golf-courses winding through the desert, dozens of them, even the fairways seeming to be clipped with nail scissors. On a hill is a mass of rusty iron girders. Bob Hope's house, which went on fire while he was building it. He walked away from the

160

wreckage and built another one. Sinatra's house, now sold, is buried in a mile-long forest of palm trees. Money seems to hang in the air in even greater profusion than the dates.

All over California people live in bungalows tucked tightly into the landscape. From the outside they look like nothing. Inside, the rooms are huge with plate-glass windows framing views of the Pacific, the desert or thousands of miles of barren mountains and yet another manicured golf-course. Everything works beautifully. Gardeners arrive with trucks filled with lawnmowers and the other tools of their trade. Young men with long hair clean your pool. The daily maid arrives in a station-wagon about thirty feet long. And the sky is a burning blue every single day in the year.

It glares down, too, on Las Vegas, which is really only round the corner by air, but it's hard to get into the sun.

No one goes to Vegas to get a tan but only to gamble and drink and get into trouble and then begin all over again.

We spent forty-eight hours there, which felt like a lifetime, but from which I was able to gather only the following, fragmented notes:

(1) It is physically dangerous to approach any of the porters at Las Vegas Airport, with a request for their assistance, because they all belong to different unions and if you get the

wrong union they become derisive and finally angry, threatening you with their barrows. The visitor cannot assess the odds against winning the right union because he cannot understand one single, infinitesimal part of what's going on.

(2) There is a young policeman who stands outside the terminal building watching hundreds of people scrambling haphazardly into taxis through all four doors, having lost their friends and their luggage, being intent only upon getting to the gaming tables, and he says, 'Nobody don't do nuttin' right round he-ah.'

(3) When a gentleman arrives with two lady companions at the hotel of their choice there is an excitable young man behind the desk who cries, oblivious to the sex-war, woman's liberation and the male and female genders, 'Hello, there, you guys – great to seeyah!'

(4) There are 34,000 hotels and lodging houses in Las Vegas, and in all of them it is impossible to remain in the bedrooms for more than three to four hours. The walls are made of cardboard and the other residents, above, below and on either side, are either getting up or going to bed continuously throughout every twenty-four hours. You can hear the man next door squeezing out toothpaste. This system serves to get the customers out of bed and back to the slot machines with the shortest possible intermission.

(5) Every bedroom has colour television, the colours being bright red and bright yellow, with inaudible sound, so you're not going to sit around looking at that, either, so get back and do you work on the slots.

(6) In blazing November sunshine, with majestic views of sierras and desert, there is one – out of 34,000 chances – rooftop restaurant, because no one ought to be looking at the scenery when they might be playing blackjack. For this same reason, in 85° of searing heat, it is impossible to eat or have a drink out of doors.

(7) In none of the 34,000 casinos is there a public clock in case a crap shooter suddenly sees it's seven o'clock in the morning and decides it's bedtime, despite the fact that he hasn't, as yet, had lunch.

(8) There is a casino called Dirty Sally's into which an eighteen stone cab driver, who has seen active service in both the American Army and Navy, is afraid to enter after 2 a.m.

(9) There is another cab driver who has stood for Governor of Nevada three times, and is still driving a cab.

(10) There is a slot machine – there are millions of slot machines – that tell you put in 'one to five coins'. You pull the handle once and nothing happens, except that a sign lights up saying 'Insert coin'. You put in another five coins, pull the handle and a cascade of nickels clatters out and you realize that you've multiplied your winnings by five.

(11) There is a plastic cup beside each machine in which you store your nickels and then you try to get rid of them because both hands are black and you've got tennis-elbow in the right arm and you want to go to bed and with the very last coin you get another cursed cascade and you run round hundreds of machines, crushing in more and more nickels, pulling the handles more and more wildly until at last you're broke, and free.

(12) It is 2/1-on, in the casinos of Las Vegas, that the next woman who passes, wearing slacks, will have an even bigger bottom than the previous three hundred. The aggregate weight, at any given moment of the day or night, of female bottoms, is exactly one million tons.

(13) Towards the end of November, 1975, in the Flamingo Hilton casino, a slender-bottomed female cashed in three rolls of nickels, still wrapped, unplayed. Despite almost armed intervention on the part of the management, who had not seen this happen since Las Vegas began, she insisted on receiving dollar bills, on the grounds that the tedium of shoving nickels into slot machines was driving her mad.

(14) That was no gambler. That was my wife.

Spaghetti Junction

One really has to admire any railway system, anywhere in the world, whose first instinct upon seeing a potential passenger approach it is to make it so difficult for him to get aboard what he thinks is the right train that he will go away, after a minimal exchange of insult, never to enter a railway station ever again.

Any reputable railway system's second instinct is, if by some unfortunate confusion a passenger does get into one of their trains, to bung him into the corridor of an already overfilled second class coach, despite his first class ticket, and throw his luggage in after him so that he can sit on that if he can find a place to put it.

It's all such a bold, original, swashbuckling road to inevitable bankruptcy that one can only believe it to be a subtle camouflage for some quite different enterprise like, perhaps, persuading the Government that railways don't work, being too big and noisy and awkward, and that therefore it's high time the Government invented something else, while retaining the services of everyone employed by the previous disaster.

The British, of course, have suffered by the teething problems of this movement but, at least, they're being buffeted around in their own language, so that they can guess approximately what horrors can lie ahead through the purchase of a nice single ticket from Paddington to, say, Maidenhead. But let them try it from Antibes, France, to Genoa, Italy, five returns with seven pieces of heavy luggage, and they'll get the rough side of the once friendly little puff-puff.

First of all, the ticket distributor in Antibes doesn't just take the relevant piece of pasteboard from the rack behind him and give it to you in exchange for money. He *writes out* your ticket for you, with five pieces of carbon paper, by hand, watched by a colleague who should be doing something else. When you get it the ticket, with an increasingly dim reproduction through the carbons, looks like a claim for a double rebate on capital gains, a bonus you could conceivably get if you knew whom to send it. The ticket writer writes very slowly, with frequent reference to time-tables and ledgers, pausing as often to tell you that you're very liable to miss the train seeing that you've given him all this work to do without prior notice.

On this occasion, however, all five of us got aboard the train and into the seats we'd actually booked, with our luggage piled high on top of us, with ample time to spare, before the train left, late, owing to rumours of industrial dispute.

The rumours became reality in Ventimiglia, the first station in Italy, where we were shifted into a siding and left to wait for almost two hours while the strike was settled either there or in Rome or Milan or even Moscow. From time to time we shouted enquiries out of the windows in French, to be answered in incomprehensible, corrosive Italian – a far cry from the jocular exchanges, under similar circumstances, in the marshalling yards at Crewe.

Eventually, the French and Italian railways let us get to Genoa, very late, but obviously feeling disgraced by this weakness they let us have it, hip and thigh, on the way back to Antibes.

In Genoa they allowed us to book five seats, but only as far as Ventimiglia, where we had to change coaches, seeing that ours was rushing on to Bordeaux. We understood the ticket office to tell us we had three minutes for this transfer so we had all our luggage piled up beside the door as we pulled into Ventimiglia where, on the way out, we had spent two leisurely hours in the sidings. With the help of a very old panting porter and a lot of shouting from imperious uniformed officials we fell into a carriage at the very end of the train. And into a compartment occupied only by a charming Italian lady who expressed her surprise, mercifully in French, at all this rushing around which had left us so *bouleversés*. She, she said, had merely got into this compartment in Genoa, which was empty and had remained so until now. Furthermore, it would stop at Antibes, just before her departure at Cannes. A real uppercut by Italian railways, leaving us hanging on the ropes.

They had another savage blow in store. While we were getting all our luggage together after Menton all the lights in our carriage went out, leaving us in pitch darkness, specially in the numerous tunnels. We moved and stacked luggage by feel. The lights came on again just before Antibes where, upon arrival, we threw our stuff out on to the very furthest end of the platform, at the very moment when it began to rain. We found a porter, with a barrow, miles away in a shelter on the other side of the track, and got home in the end by taxi.

How good it felt to be motoring again.

All aboard Bala-Rama

At a time when all persons of any sense whatever are seriously thinking of taking to their beds, locking the door on the inside and filling the rest of the house with man-eating police dogs, making some kind of attempt, however feeble, to prevent themselves being mugged, blown up or kidnapped, Madame was taking me boating.

We were going boating off the coast of Turkey – an enterprise which seemed to me to be on a par with taking a canoe trip to Dunkirk, during the evacuation.

We were not alone in this madness. Two other yachters were coming from Philadelphia and two more from Maine and we were all meeting in Athens, if we didn't get hi-jacked to Peru.

From Athens we were to fly to the island of Samos, if the plane didn't get sabotaged into a million pieces. If, that was, we left Athens at all, because for all I knew the Colonels might well have been on the very edge of staging another *coup d'état* and the whole city about to burst into flames almost immediately after our arrival.

On the island of Samos, we were to board – if it hadn't sprung a leak – a fifty-three foot clipper ketch called *Bala-Rama II*, where we were assured that at least we should have no language problems because the owner-skipper spoke Turkish, English, American and Greek. Then we untied the string and sailed into the middle of the Russian Navy, pouring out of the Black Sea, shadowed by the US Sixth Fleet, with a flotilla of Turkish destroyers making purposefully for Cyprus under the guns of Greek dreadnoughts while two British naval motor-boats – the whole Mediterranean complement – tried to get out of the way.

In those churning seas it didn't seem to me that there'd be enough water left over on which *Bala-Rama II* could float.

And it was small comfort that the owner-skipper spoke Turkish, English, American and Greek. Where was his Russian, then? How was he going to explain that we weren't a Q-ship, bursting with Polaris missiles, when we were surrounded by six Russian submarines?

These Russian jitters were new. They came on after I looked at the map and saw that the Black Sea, full of Russians, goes for miles and miles along the northern coast of Turkey. I never knew they were so near. And, what's more, looking at the map, I saw that we were not only going to be knee-deep in Russians, during this gentle pleasure cruise along the Turkish coast, but that also we would be within rowing distance of the civil war in the Lebanon, to say nothing of Syria, liable to get bombed at any moment by the Israeli Air Force, disturbing our lunch.

And another thing. Having further reference to the map I noted that the island of Rhodes stood four-square across our path from Samos. Unless the owner-skipper of *Bala-Rama II* kept a pretty sharp lookout we'd probably run straight into it. But who owned Rhodes? What was the political situation like there? Were there, perhaps, radical elements on the island who had it deeply in for Protestant Southern

Irishmen and if so in what painful forms did they tend to express their animosity?

Suddenly – and it was much too late – I realized I didn't know anything at all about South Western Asia. In fact, I didn't even know it was called South Western Asia until I looked at the map which I wished so sincerely I had never seen.

Take Turkey itself. Democracy? Military government? Stable? Unstable? Who was the boss, if they had one? Surely the Greeks had been on the edge of invading it for years? If they did so within the next two weeks who was going to win and how far out to sea were the repercussions liable to be felt? And as if all these worries weren't enough I'd also got the problem of which trousers and what woollies to bring.

There was probably a bitter Turkish wind called the *poush-poush* that came snoring out of the Dardenelles, freezing a man wearing light trousers to death within a matter of minutes. And, like as not, the *poush-poush* was followed instantly by the *moosh-moosh*, howling off the deserts of Syria like the breath of Hell.

The extraordinary thing is that the others were looking forward with a child-like eagerness to this probably fatal expedition.

They talked dreamily about 'simply lolling around in that heavenly turquoise sea'. But then, of course, they were entirely unaware of the political dynamite that is South Western Asia.

Before I did any lolling around in that heavenly turquoise sea I was going to make sure there were no periscopes about . . .

This nervous yachtsman would have been unrecognizable a week later, lolling about on skins in Ali Guven's sandal shop in Bodrum, drinking Turkish beer from bottles, if that's what it was.

Bodrum is a wild little yachting-fishing-boatbuilding port about halfway down the south-west coast of Turkey, guarded by an immense castle-museum with a low-slung black and white dog that shows you around the exhibits.

Ali Guven, by the concensus of local opinion, is the world's greatest sandal maker. He is certainly something special himself.

Pale, startling eyes, greying beard, *farouche* in the extreme. He's got an assistant with teeth made of living alabaster. I think Ali's name is Guven, because that's what he stamps on his sandals. It might mean 'Pure Leather' or 'Made in Turkey'. Hard to say, really, because Ali(?) speaks only Turkish. Admittedly, the living alabaster tooth-man speaks English but he couldn't get a word in edgeways because Peter and Ali were really going at it, in the native tongue.

Peter Dibonas, born in Lithuania, French father, Lit mother, now naturalized American and owner of the *Bala-Rama II*, based in Bodrum, naturally enough speaks fluent

Turkish, in addition to being able to ride a bicycle, touch type, drive a car, handle a horse and look like – good luck to him – a golden haired young Viking, whilst simultaneously being able to take a star-shot and repair the engine of his boat. Just the kind of lad you'd like to take home.

Well, there we all were rapping away in various languages when suddenly Elspeth had to climb in through the open window to avoid a lorry thundering down the narrow street. That's Elspeth Campbell (no relation), a splendid chunky little girl from Argyllshire who is cook and deckhand aboard Peter's boat. In the past ten days she had made breakfast, lunch and dinner for ten people without putting a spoon wrong, communicating with Able Seaman Mehmet in French, which he speaks in addition to his native Turkish, and with Captain Erdoine in sign language, because he speaks only Turkish and Greek.

At this range it seems to be impossible to guess what we were all laughing at, in three languages. No. It was four, because there was a pretty young German girl sitting on a stool just inside the door and I was chatting her up in German, despite a forty-year gap in my use of the same and despite, too, her resolute use of impeccably accented English in reply.

At this moment Olaf, a leathery, bearded old Scandinavian wearing shorts, together with the fairly unusual accessories of one

173

green wooden clog and one red one, shepherded his new dog past the door – a puppy perhaps six inches long. It was lucky he didn't come in – not that there was room for him – or we might have had to add medieval Norse to the conversation.

Like Peter Dibonas, he too lives in Bodrum, like François with the concrete boat and the German youth with the orange-red hair in his huge steel thing. They all have the air of perfect contentment, while the tape-recorded voice of the muezzin howls in what seems like despair from the tapering tower of the mosque.

Turkey is really extraordinary. We cruised for six hundred miles up and down this rocky coastline, under blazing blue skies, scarcely ever seeing another human being, a house or a boat. Mile after mile of stony mountains, entirely devoid of human kind, and then at night swinging into a tiny, land-locked bay with forests of bright-green fir trees coming down to the water's edge, the only sound, as the sun went down, the alarming screaming of a jackal, somewhere in the woods.

Apart, of course, from the noise we were making ourselves. *Bala-Rama II*, lit up like a block of flats, with Beethoven's Third booming from the stereophonic speakers and the roar of six European and American voices taking a little vod and ton before din-dins. Anchor down and the stern line round a fir tree, *Bala-Rama II* sat motionlessly on a sea of black glass, swallowed up – despite the music and the bellow of intellectual discussion – by the silence of pre-Christian times.

In any other part of the Mediterranean we would have been jammed hull to hull in some marina, with the boat next door pumping out its bilges and the mariners on the other side having a party with guitars. The green fir trees would long since have given way to high-rise hotels and discotheques and phony restaurants, with the bottom of the sea hidden for ever by the effluents of man.

Obviously, the bare stony mountains and the lack of roads will prevent us using this magical, dazzling silence for quite some time – to its full, modern effect. Also, the ancient image of the Turk – a savage, scimitar-slashing barbarian with moustachios that would frighten a lion – might also help, momentarily, to keep civilization at bay.

Until, of course, one gets into Ali's shop, lying back on a pile of skins with a cold beer, philosophizing in a language one doesn't speak.

That's when the real Turkey comes through.

Coming ashore from yachting our sea-legs were still a little wobbly as we rolled into the hotel in Athens, but they stiffened like steel springs when Reception said they had no reservations in our name.

Substantial shouting broke out upon the moment. Absolutely inconceivable idiocy. Booking made months ago. The incredible incompetence of hotels all over the world. Illiterate clerks. Ham-handed management. At this point we found we were in the wrong hotel. The one next door was waiting for us with open arms and a complimentary basket of fruit.

We took the first baths we'd had in ten days, surprised by the deposits laid upon us by the open sea and sky, and then – at 11 a.m. – lay down for a short rest before lunch, for which we were ready, seeing that we'd had no breakfast. When we woke, at 5.25 p.m., we hadn't had any lunch, either.

We savaged the management's complimentary basket of fruit and sat down to make plans for dinner.

The place to dine is the Plaka, the Athenian equivalent of Soho, in London. We had often dined in the Plaka before, much enjoying the traditional plate-breaking and dancing with waiters, wrists bound to wrists with table-napkins. But just in case the old place had changed we consulted a guide book, which revealed that currently the most fashionable restaurant in the Plaka was the Xynos, in Thespidos street. We decided to walk there, seeing that not much happens in Athens before 8 p.m.

Not being sure of the pronunciation of Xynos which, whatever it might be in reality, certainly was nothing like 'Exinos', we plotted our path on the map with extreme care. Straight down Leoforos Amalias to

Hadrian's Arch, turn right up Lissikratous street and there before our very eyes would be Thespidos street and the currently most fashionable restaurant in the Plaka, however it was pronounced in Greek.

We strode out of the hotel. Briskly, Madame turned to the left. With equal confidence I turned to the right. We went back into the hotel again where she reopened the map with a certain crispness. 'There you are,' she said. 'Left.' I said, 'I'm awfully sorry, but I'm almost sure it's right.' 'Very well, I shall follow you.'

This, of course, was a hopeless proposition, because she bursts from the trap with the speed of an odds-on greyhound whilst I always begin with a certain amount of wheel-spin. This leaves me, always and everywhere, panting along fifty yards behind.

She was waiting for me at the first crossing. 'Where now?' I looked up at the name of the street. The usual Greek ragbag of letters looking like open-ended rectangles, A's with crossbars and A's without, M's lying on their sides, M's the right way up, O's with strokes underneath them and even right through their middle. 'Straight on, I think.'

Half an hour later we were in the Plaka, all right, but interred in the Plaka, buried up to our necks in pandemonium of discotheques, blaring out *Greek* hard rock, beset by touts, three-year-old shoeshine boys and ladies who were, probably, of the night.

By this time I'd learnt, from a young policeman dripping with artillery, that the restaurant was called 'Zeenos', but he probably misunderstood me because he added, 'You in it now.' We were standing outside a nightclub inside which seven banshees were trying to burst their instruments, in blood-red light. When we found the Xynos, in a quiet garden, we found it was fully booked not only for tonight but for several weeks ahead. We took to the stricken streets again, taxi horns screaming at us, banshees blaring, touts plucking at our sleeves. When we found the Taverna we fell into it, simply because it was empty, save for two ladies in close consultation and a step-ladder leaning against the wall. But then three exuberant Greek gentlemen burst out of the back of the premises and seized us with love by our hands, arms, shoulders and necks. 'You look downstairs,' they cried in unison. 'It fairy nice.'

It *was* fairy nice. An empty cellar plastered with murals of salmon-pink, stark-naked gods and goddesses, a giant bulging Bacchus playing a lively part as one and all sported in fields of livid green. 'Fairy nice,' we said, 'but fairy nicer upstairs.'

We had an adequate dinner of grilled prawns and salad, to the surprised delight of the proprietors, two bottles of Demestica white wine. It cost £7 – even if it did exclude plate-breaking and the pleasures of the napkin dance.

We asked them how to get back to the hotel. 'Down street,' they cried, 'left turn, you there.' We there in ten minutes, when the outward journey had taken us an hour and a half.

In the lifetime we spent in the Plaka we never once saw the floodlit Parthenon, at the feet of which the Plaka lies.

Perhaps it's been pulverized by the noise.

Sempre diretto

The roughest aspect of this simple, speedy drive to Venice was breakfast at 5.40 a.m. in pitch darkness, with stars somewhat feeble in a dank overcast. Not too much ostentatious chattering during this spread, but gracious smiles for Sandy and Greg as we picked them up at their house and added their baggage to ours.

We had two suitcases, one large zip bag, three small zip bags, one large canvas bag, a straw basket, a pink and white chequered ice-box, two mackintoshes, two fur coats and an anorak – all essential equipment for the experienced traveller.

We slipped through sleeping Nice like bananas off a hot shovel and as we mounted the Moyenne Corniche to the begining of the autostrada above Ventimiglia dawn burst through the dank overcast, as refulgent as our pink and white ice-box. It went again immediately, overwhelmed by a bitter wind and cloud the colour of dirty ice. Against this dingy backdrop the yellow light suddenly shining from the dashboard, indicating a probably short circuit in the generator, looked like a miniature sun.

Sure it would get better I sped on, over the frontier, but yielded to the passengers' animated suggestion at the next garage but four. Sandy, with a grip on the Italian language, got out to explain things to a young mechanic. I followed him and became aware that someone was pumping something up with a compressor – an angry, windy sound. Then I saw that the nearside front tyre was pumping itself down, suffering from some inconceivable puncture.

When we left the garage we had the punctured tyre under the bonnet, the spare wheel on, a tube of glue to blow into it if it went flat, some majic booster in the battery, heavy rain falling and the yellow light shining bravely from the dashboard. The speedy, simple drive to Venice was gathering some implications.

When we entered the outskirts of Genoa we found they had torn up the former autostrada or were rebuilding it or turning it back to front or constructing looping viaducts to pass high above the whole city. In heavy rain we splashed through builders' yards, pot-holed slipways and emergency lanes, to climb away from this disaster area through an interminable series of endless tunnels, so dimly illuminated inside that by comparison the yellow dashboard light was dazzling.

It was snowing, on the other side of the tunnels. With the help of fog visibility was down to perhaps one hundred yards. For an hour Italian drivers, for mile upon mile of dead-straight autostrada, whipped past, spraying us with mud, despite the fact that I was piloting our gondola at seventy-five mph.

I pulled into a lay-by, somewhere in the middle of the muddy, snowy, utterly desolate plains of Lombardy. The only feature we could see was a low, wire fence beside us, hung with wind-swept paper and rags. We took some refreshment. Greg said, voicing her life-long passion for Venice, 'Think of that beautiful sun on the Campanile.' I turned on the ignition again. Our own little sun smiled gallantly back.

Another one hundred and fifty miles, windows steamed inside, snowy horrors out-side, but unpunctured, I stopped in the forecourt of another garage, for lunch. Upper bracket feeding – smoked salmon on pumper-nickel bread, stuffed eggs, champagne and strengthened coffee to follow. After that the car wouldn't start, because the battery was flat.

Sandy arranged a squirt from another battery. As we sped off again he said, in his happy, innocent way, 'Isn't it lucky we're always in a garage when something goes wrong.'

We arrived in Venice in drenching rain, having seen nothing but water, sleet, snow and mud. Just inside the portals of the municipal garage we ran out of petrol, and stopped dead, repeating our winning feat. While Sandy arranged repairs, to be done during the coming week, the ladies and I unloaded the two suitcases, the one large zip bag, the three small zip bags and the rest of our essentials and after a long, slow-motion dance got them and ourselves aboard a motor-launch, which left us at the landing-stage beside the Gritti Palace Hotel.

Ahead of us was a passage as wide as myself, leading to our apartments just behind the Hotel, in the Plazzo del Giglio. We loaded ourselves like pack mules. Two young girls came out of the alley. We got into it. Two young men were in there, trying to follow the girls. Then the girls tried to rejoin the young men. After an altercation in French, English and Italian we shoved the young men ahead of us into the square in front of our apartment, fending off the girls trying to get in our way. The rain redoubled itself as the young people joined forces yet again, making surprising gestures at the shattered travellers.

That night we walked round the corner to

the Colomba Restaurant, blissfully deprived of wheels and broken mechanism, each of us glowing with a private little yellow light.

For a week after that we strolled through picturesque little *Campi*, which I believe to be small Venetian squares, through *Piazzi*, which are bigger ones, over *Ponti* (bridges?) and seventy-three times through the Piazzo San Marco.

The major work in strolling through Venice is peering round the next corner, wondering if this is the alley that goes to the Rialto or will possibly rebury us in the echoing corridors of the labyrinthine hospital. Once we got stuck in here for so long that I became exhausted to the point of unconsciousness and had to lean against a peeling wall waiting for the world to slow down, and to steady itself again. Two orderlies in white, pushing a kind of wheelbarrow, gave me a narrow look, as though estimating that they had another client. I broke away from them, in dread, and found my exit barred by a high iron gate, padlocked and double bolted. They were right on my trail as I fought my way out into the nearest alleyway, which turned out to be a *cul de sac*. In comparison with Venice the Hampton Court maze is a football ground.

In Venice there is no point in asking the way to the Piazza San Marco or the Rialto or anywhere else, because the indigenous citizens, centuries ago, gave up handing out explicit instructions – such as, 'First right, then the third on the left, over the next bridge, then right, two more left turns, another bridge – the smaller of the two – then right again . . .' What they say is, '*Sempre diretto*', which probably means 'Straight ahead', and into the sea.

Many of these expeditions culminated in the purchasing of food and drink for the nourishment of our two apartments at the back of the Gritti Palace Hotel. Extreme comfort, two charming maids, a butler-porter and a completely equipped kitchen the size of a yacht's galley. In some curious way all four of us seemed, individually, to buy exactly the same comestibles so that both kitchens were so filled with food and drink that we had to slam the doors to keep it all inside. One veal stew was so large that it lasted us for three days and three nights, and the straw basket and the large canvas bag were so tightly packed with bottles that we could scarcely make an impression on them, try as we might. By *force majeure* every afternoon confined us to bed, preparatory to the evening stroll round the corner, over the small bridge, first left, two right turns, and straight ahead possibly into the Piazza San Marco or the wooden bridge over the Grand Canal, whichever came up first.

When, therefore, we came to say farewell to Serenissima, to drive home again to France, it was decided that we would stay the night in Turin, on the grounds that all four of us would be fast asleep by 3.30 p.m. It was an hour and a half after our bedtime when we crept into that beautiful, medieval city and became, instantly, lost.

All the streets in Turin are one-way, some of them, apparently, in both directions. We were almost mangled by a tram and finished off by a bus at one congested crossing, so that when in the end we found our hotel I was glad to hand the car over to a functionary in a peaked cap and someone else's overcoat, who offered to put it away in the garage. He began by reversing, looking over his shoulder, and shot forward almost into the foyer, before sorting out the gear box.

A stern Italian behind the desk gave us two slips of paper containing the numbers of our rooms, with far bigger numbers underneath. No less than 47,000 lira per chamber, plus twelve per cent VAT plus – if you please – another lump of VAT at six per cent, making a grand total of 54,371 lira per night – or about £30 for the use of two beds and a bath. In the month of February, in a city like Turin. After the lira had been devalued by ten per cent.

We asked the Generalissimo behind the desk if he could recommend a restaurant for dinner. 'All restaurant here shut on Sunday or bankrupt,' he said grimly. 'You eat here.'

When we entered the restaurant eight waiters were waiting on two commercial travellers at separate tables. We ordered hors

185

d'oeuvres and a bottle of wine, to begin with. The hors d'oeuvres turned out to be vinegar with some strips of pink rubber lying in it. We told the head waiter we proposed to terminate dinner at this point. He was kind enough to give me a bill for £10.

Next morning, when presented with the account, I found I'd been charged £1 for ice in the bedroom, and £2 for a bottle of beer. The garage functionary asked £2 for the safe-keeping of the car and three porters settled for a quid a nob for handling the luggage.

When we drove away from Turin we discovered that the four of us had left behind, in aggregate, the sum of £100 for a night's lodging.

Before I learn to speak Italian in the *Mafiosi vernaculare* I shall not be going back to Torino again.

Do you remember an inn?

I got whirled away for commercial purposes suddenly to Paris and into a discreetly luxurious hotel the outside of which I have admittedly seen before but always from the other side of the street.

It is one of those hotels into which men with real-leather, extra-slim, combination-locked briefcases are always bustling with the indelible aura of executives who are working on their expenses with such skill and diligence that they might just as well have left their own wallets at home, having extracted and put in a secure pocket those credit cards which they know to be viable in the field of their coming manoeuvres. When they come bustling out their aura is notably pinker and meatier than when they bustled in because naturally enough they have not stinted themselves inside with the foods and other refreshments seeing that their only physical contribution to the payment for same has been the signing, somewhat illegibly, of whatever bills may have been placed in front of them.

This is why I only observe this hotel from the other side of the street, in case a sudden friendship breaks out with one or more of the briefcase gentlemen and I am swept with them into the bar, where the first couple of rounds will be paid for by their companies and the third one by me, leaving my purse looking like a burst balloon.

But now, in Paris, I was in a position of no little power, being a guest of the parties of the first part who, according to a morning-suited operative behind the hotel desk, were still, owing to travel problems, in London.

In a word, I had the run of my teeth in

this discreetly luxurious hotel until about 8.30 p.m. and obviously, by business convention, expected to let them have as active a time as they could provide. And yet, I was not entirely free because wherever I looked I saw signs stating, '15% service not included'. That was a proper yorker. Any entanglement with the staff, on these terms, would rupture my financial empire, already in a skinny condition owing to the speed with which I'd been whipped, entirely unprepared, from home.

Fortunately, the morning-suited operative was kind enough to carry my overnight bag upstairs to my bedroom all by himself. Rather than embarrass him – and even more myself – by the exchange of a note or two I paid him in lavish thanks, interwoven with compliments upon the exquisite taste of the furniture and the bed. He must have heard a lot of this evasive stuff before because he withdrew before I could reach the subject of the absolutely delightful curtains, leaving me – I found almost immediately – in sole charge of a small refrigerator packed with miniature bottles of spirits, several brands of beers and minerals and two bottles of very good champagne. On top of the fridge was a price list for every item of merchandise within, with instructions to tick off anything consumed and present it to the manager before departure.

With a curious sense of guilt I extracted a bottle of lager – £1.50 – and poured some of it

into a very small glass found in the bathroom –
no service required, thank you very much
indeed. I then added up the cost of the
emptying the fridge, in its entirety, down my
throat and came up with a total of very nearly
£75. In all conscience not an immediately
justifiable expense.

About an hour later, and one lager ahead of
the game, I decided it was time to spend some
of my own resources, so I went down to the
bar. At a strategic table near the entrance were
a couple of thick-set clients in the height of
informal wear sharing a whole bottle of
whiskey which, by its label, I could tell was at
least twelve years old. I ordered a Dubonnet,
with a slice of lemon and a cube or two of ice.
The barman added a slip of paper requesting
the payment of £3.30, service not included. I
dallied over my drink, waiting for the ice to
melt so I could have that too, calculating that
if mine had been £3.30 the bottle of whiskey
would have been in the region of £50. Some
aperitif before dinner.

I then went to the concierge's desk and
asked a most amiable young man to straighten
out, by telephone, some complexities in my
airline ticket. He performed this service so
well and so quickly that I slipped him £4. It
should probably have been a fiver, but I was
keeping one for myself just in case. I had
recourse, next, to the cash desk with a cheque
books, passport, driving licence and two
credit cards as proof of identity, to be told that

cheques could only be cashed by permission of the Director, who was not there. I said, with some fire, that they were probably not accustomed to the sight of actual money but in the last half hour I'd poured £7.30 in cash into the hotel so could I have it back, by cheque. The answer was no, by the plainer of the two girls who up till now had been handling my case.

I asked her why. Why no?

'Because cheques can only be cashed by permission—'

'—of the Director who is not here.' I remembered that bit, but wanted to get into some new material. 'When the Director goes away,' I suggested, 'he must surely leave some deputy behind to handle his many duties. One who can read and spell.'

The prettier one took over. They were a well-trained team. At some length, with lovely teeth, she explained that transactions of this kind always made problems for hotels. For emphasis she transferred from French into English. 'There are many naughtee people about,' she said.

'Apart from you,' I said, 'they are all in hotels.'

She smiled, raising her shoulders a milli-metre or two to indicate that while there might possibly be something in such a contention it was no part of her duties to be pro or con.

★

The next time I was in an hotel it was in London, in a drawing-room suite, once again being paid for by somebody else. Nonetheless I was waiting with impatience for something to stir down in the service forest.

Exactly fifteen minutes before, I had pressed the stirring bell with the utmost delicacy, that gossamer touch that says to anyone who might possibly be interested, 'I'm fearfully sorry to disturb you, but if you're not doing anything else could you drop in here for a single second so that I can present you with a small commission which will take you no time at all, and an absolute minimum of physical effort to fulfil, thank you very very much indeed.'

There had been no answer to that courteous appeal.

Some time later, running at it, I pushed the bell almost through the wall and into the room next door, holding it there in trembling rage. This is the call for room service that says, 'Get up here, ratface, in three seconds or I'm gonna come down and getcha!'

There had been no reply to that one either.

It was then, in a kind of vision, that I saw how room service is recruited, and trained, for the modern hotel.

As personnel manager I am standing at the back door of our palace, keeping an eye out for the raw material of staff, seeing that seventy-two per cent of my existing lads have disappeared overnight, one of them taking a whole carpet with him.

My needs are small. I want a bunch of males under eighty years of age who can walk in a fairly straight line without falling down. As yet, they do not have to know how to carry a tray. All that kind of polish can be applied later.

I require them to be of a nationality whose native tongue is so obscure as to be unplaceable even by polyglot guests, ranging through French, Spanish, Italian, Greek and German, in search of a box of matches or a ham sandwich. This will ensure that the waiter, trying English, will be hermetically incomprehensible to the customers, nor will he understand a single word that is addressed to him in any conceivable language under the sun. This, of course, will in no way impede his activities in the guest rooms or the corridors, in that he can gallop up and down all day long without being slowed by knowing what he's supposed to be doing.

My staff course begins with breakfast, a meal that can bring the guests to heel at the very beginning of the day. I show them one of the forms upon which I have noted the ingredients of breakfast for two: i.e. one Continental Breakfast, with China tea and a slice of lemon, and one Full Breakfast, with orange juice, two eggs, bacon, toast and coffee. I point out to them that there is no need for them even to be able to understand the punctuation in this order form. All they have to do is to give it to the chef. But, I

192

hasten to emphasize, when the chef gives them the tray this is when their work begins.

Not a word of these instructions has come through to them. Two of them are even playing a complicated card game that might be Serbo-Croatian belote, or Latvian snap. I am not put out because, having before me six sample breakfasts, I can show them, visually, what I want them to do. Namely, to change all the ingredients of all the breakfasts around so that no single guest gets anything in the least like what he originally ordered. That is, the Continental Breakfast might come out as cocoa, kippers and fruit salad, whilst the Full Breakfast result in a rusk and a glass of buttermilk. Furthermore, everyone who has ordered *The Times* gets the *Sun*, and vice versa.

At this point I ask them if anyone speaks English. Everyone instantly raises a hand. They understand that one, but of course nothing else. Nonetheless, I address them in a slow, careful voice. 'When bell rings wait half-hour before answering. Then bring breakfast when man – or, preferably, young woman – in bath. Or guests have gone out to find breakfast somewhere else. Right, lads – trial run.'

I ring a bell. The Latvian snap turns into a six-hander. Three of them start eating the sample breakfasts. One puts on his overcoat and leaves, as it turns out, for good. Pretty well perfect. . .

At this point my own bell was actually answered. A young man came into the room in an off-white coat, his hands concealed by the sleeves. I ordered a bottle of vodka, six tomato juice and six tonic. He gave me a stern look, and left.

In the following twenty minutes I had another vision. I saw what the modern hotel is trying to do: to wit, to make room service so incurably slovenly that the staff can be got rid of in its entirety, leaving the guests to get off their fat bottoms and do a bit for themselves.

My runner in these stakes came back at this moment with, in place of my order, one bottle of tomato juice, one tonic and a very small vodka in a rather dirty wine-glass.

A perfect move, one guaranteed to galvanize the guests into action.

Flying the box

Even if they'd turned out to be the last few drops of juice the sheiks had ever let us have the trip would have been worth it, just for the laughs alone.

The whole thing lasted for thirteen and a half hours, and I was laughing continuously the whole time.

Got the first rib-tickler as we rose from Manchester Airport at 8 a.m., *with the Captain sitting beside me.* There he was as large as life, covered in gold bars with his fruit-salad cap on his knee, leaving the tiresome business of take-off to some lop-eared lad up front. I was chuckling quite a bit as I said to him, 'Don't quite feel up to driving her this morning, eh, Skip?'

He broke into a great roar of laughter. 'I'm not the Captain,' he sobbed, 'not on this flight. I'm only going down to the box in London.'

I wiped my eye in turn. When I could speak I said, 'But you *are* a British Airways captain and now you're going into a loony bin in London?'

Handkerchiefs out for both of us and then he explained that 'the box' was the simulated flight test taken by pilots every six months. He showed me a page of his homework. Simulated flight taking off from Dusseldorf, port engine goes on fire, partial electrical failure, nose-wheel jammed down, small explosion in the galley, etc. Holding my sides, I said, 'Has it ever happened to you?' He fair rattled our coffee cups as he replied, 'Not yet.'

An hour and a half later – scheduled flying time to London, thirty minutes – we landed at Gatwick, with aching ribs. Fog at Heathrow, only one runway, etc. 'I'll be late for school,' he said, holding on to a pillar,

'I'll get the sack.' 'I'll miss the 10.45 to Nice,' I said, bent double, 'and there isn't another one until tomorrow.' We parted, hooting.

The coach, speeding from Gatwick to Heathrow, got stuck in a traffic jam in Reigate. I said to the man beside me, 'Great way of getting from Manchester to Nice,' doubling up all over again. He nearly split himself. 'For me,' he said, 'Buenos Aires.' We had to hold on to one another as we passed through Coulsdon, Ewell, Walton-on-the-Hill, etc.

At the British Airways desk in Terminal One the girl nearly did herself an injury. 'Your plane to Nice is still here,' she said, 'but they've shut the door so you can't get into it.' I had to use my coatsleeve. 'I could ride outside?' Eventually she was able to gasp out, 'You could get into Air Iran, going to Paris. But don't forget to get out because it's going on to Teheran.'

I staggered into a bus that left me at Terminal Three, where everyone else was going to Los Angeles, Sydney, Hong Kong, Teheran, etc. Except for the TWA passengers, who weren't going anywhere, because of a lightning strike by the cabin staff.

As I looked at the Departure Board the departure time for Air Iran to Paris changed from 12.45 to 2.30, putting me right back in the chuckling field again. Still laughing like mad I gave my duty-free loot back to the Customs, de-emigrated myself and went upstairs to the restaurant, where the maître d'hôtel tried to force lunch on me at the expense of TWA. We soaked a napkin each when I showed him my Air Iran boarding card. I'd just ordered an expensive bottle of wine, on me, when a Pan-Am executive arrived and said, 'My dear sir, how nice to see you again. Off to New York? Have lunch with us.' After he'd added a lovely Rémy-Martin and paid the bill I explained I was rather more aiming at Paris, than New York, and both of us laughed our heads off.

We were searched to the skin before boarding Air Iran. I tried to explain that the Shah was in no danger from me, because I was getting off in Paris, but I was laughing too much to articulate. When I arrived at Paris-Orly I found that the 5.10 p.m. to Nice was still there, but the doors were shut, and the next flight was at 7 p.m. As I looked at the Departure Board that changed to 7.30 p.m., so I had to lie down on one of the plastic sofas and waggle my legs in the air and simply howl.

On the flight from Paris to Nice I sat next to a girl in the uniform of an Air France hostess. Chuckling as usual, I asked her if she was going down to '*la boîte à Nice*'. With asperity she said she never went to night-clubs with strange men, and changed her seat.

That was the only bit I didn't tell Madame when I got home at 9.45 p.m. – ex-Manchester 8 a.m. – but we had a fair old titter over the rest.

197

The Little Outdoors

Pay-ash minoos

Of all the awkward, lumpish, recalcitrant, downright mean addictions to the *dolce (?) vita* of the *Côte d'Azur* – I don't even know, in my fury, *Welche Sprache* I'm in – a swimming-pool, continuously nine-tenths empty, is the Big Top Bastard.

I know I've been running on about this pool, a bit, lately, but it's giving me such stick I have not a second to myself in which to reflect upon religion, philosophy, politics, truth, beauty and – and that.

For some reason – and when I pin it down I'm going to begin wholesale sueing – swimming-pools attract to themselves, in the field of professional experts, men who could tie a tight knot in a steel tube merely by looking at it.

A friend of ours bought a house some time ago with a large pool in the grounds which leaked when he filled it. Four separate firms tried, and failed, to cure the leak. The fifth – a straight genius – persuaded the owner to abandon this hole and to dig another one beside it, filling in the offending one with the earth from the second. Halfway down he ran into a solid block of, apparently, granite, one hundred yards long and forty feet deep, so this friend of ours finished up with *two* half-empty pools, filled with mud, which he turned into two sunken Italian gardens, which he didn't want. All normal in the world of pools.

The charming young man who built ours went bankrupt, invalidating – in small print – his guarantee, but not before he'd had time to dig a huge hole, surrounded by mountains of yellow clay, in the garden of his next client, leaving this individual spellbound when the young man said goodbye.

When our pump failed, some years later, a pools expert wearing an *apricot-coloured wig* came and looked at it, said it was a simple matter to repair and instead of repairing it went away and was never seen again. Perhaps his wig had got sucked into the machinery of someone else's pool and he didn't want to be seen without it. All normal in the pools world.

The next man we tried attacked us savagely, shouting that in view of the fact that his firm had not built our pool even if it was lined with platinum he would not come even to look at it. The next one, wearier, said he only built pools and if anything went wrong with them it was tough *fromage* because he was too busy building new ones to be bothered with any single one of the ones he'd already built.

The third man, wearing a trendy safari suit

and curiously irrelevant half-moon glasses, arrived with his wife, who turned out to be his mind worker. He pointed at the pool and said, '*La . . . la . . .*' His wife said, '*L'eau.*' With satisfaction, the man said, '*Voilà!*' and embarked upon a new thought. '*C'est – c'est—*' '*Sale*', his wife said. Mercifully, having promised to return at 7.30 the next morning, he was not seen again, or all of us would have been standing around the fouled pool to this very day. No real break with tradition, there.

Now, we have a splendid, athletic youth who came, two hours late, to clean our filthy, empty pool with spirits of salts, instead of the allegedly more efficacious, less corrosive product that had been promised. At 6 a.m., on the morning of his arrival at 10.30, I'd pumped out the pool, partially filled, as usual, with the lashing evening rains of May, but he refilled it, to the previous level, with the hose and spent the rest of the morning trying to draw this dribble of water through the filter pump, to assess the condition of this machinery. It didn't work, nor did he come back that afternoon.

Next day, however, he cleaned the pool most beautifully with spirits of salts, handing up to me, his assistant, bucket after bucket of steaming, mephetic glue for disposal in any area of my own choice. I chose the rubbish dump, hoping it would make it go away, and scampered back with empty buckets for more.

Now he has again gone away, whilst promising to return, but leaving me in a pickle that I never would have imagined even the world of pools could brew up. For a start, he has taken with him the corroded rim from the under-water light, for re-chroming, leaving the 600-watt bulb, with its remaining fittings and rope-like cable, lying on the bottom of the pool. He has also found that the pipe which leads from the plug-hole to the filter pump is so blocked with calcium deposits that another firm will have to clear it out before, of course, the pool is refilled. On the other hand, he has advised me to refill the pool without delay, because in the heat of the sun, if any, the interior walls are going to crack. He further assures me that no harm will come from the submersion of the 600-watt bulb fitting, lying on the bottom of the shallow end of the pool

All back to normal in the world of the pool: i.e. the owner unable to move hand or foot in the absence of the expert, who may never return.

Perhaps, a really deep sunken Italian garden? Although, of course, when it comes to making holes in the ground with water in them our family never give up.

When my father was Chairman of the Great Northern Railway – trains that rushed from Belfast to Dublin and back – he constructed a swimming-pool in a stream that ran through his house or, rather, garden, outside Dublin.

He spent months of personal toil in the river bed digging up rocks and throwing them away. One day he realized that if these excavations were to continue he would have to buy a diving-suit and some kind of water-proof pneumatic drill, seeing that the boiling brown mountain river water was almost up to his waist.

Shortly after that the heavy mob moved in, carrying with them the massive ingredients of a dam, and machinery with which to make a sluice gate. The most cursory inspection revealed the presence of railway lines, sleepers and immense valves with wheels that could only have come from a locomotive. It was obvious that my father had suddenly remembered he was Chairman of the Great Northern and in a position to put his powers to good use.

He was only just in time, because the dam and the sluice gate were barely installed before the British Government nationalized the northern end of this line and the Irish Government nationalized the other bit, so that he was left with nothing to chair. But he had a beautiful little pool of pellucid brown river water in which trout sometimes joined the bathers.

Many years later, and in another country, I also had a beautiful little pool filled with brown water, but it wasn't pellucid and I didn't like to think what monstrous forms of marine life might lie beneath its murky surface.

It happened quite without warning. One

day a slight greenish tinge and the next it was as though someone had tipped in a hogshead or two of old oak stain, during the night.

We found a new pool expert, having despaired of the previous dozen. He arrived a week later, which isn't too bad for the South of France. As he came in through the gate he said we undoubtedly needed a new filter plant and he could let us have one for something rather less than a thousand pounds. Instead of that we urged him to look at the water and provide at least a theory as to how it might possibly be clarified.

He looked at the water and said, '*Pay-ash minoos, pay-ash ploos, Désalgine Eex Quarante, Chloriklar comprimés dissolution rapide, Décalcite filtre et peutêtre un coup de Piccolo Ultralong.*'

We asked if he had it with him and he said he'd left it at the factory, believing that what we really needed was this new filter, retailing at the competitive price of eight hundred and fifty quid. We said we'd settle for Pay-ash minoos and all its little friends, and could we have it this very afternoon.

Incredibly, only three days later, his wife arrived with a large cardboard box filled with plastic bottles, relieved me of a cheque for £34 and left, saying that all would now go well.

We examined the contents of the box and found that she had forgotten the Piccolo Ultralong, which was a pity, because I'd grown fond of it. We also discovered that pay-ash minoos and pay-ash ploos were PH Minus and PH Plus, although we didn't know what to do with either of them.

We spent the rest of the day reading the instructions on the bottle, and the handbook which explained the instructions. Madame, always one for direct, incisive action, said we'd begin by decalcifying the filter, and poured about half the bottle of *Décalcite filtre* into the skimmer. It went mad, foaming like detergent under high pressure.

It stopped foaming after a long time and we back-washed. Grey, turgid glue poured from the end of the hosepipe. After it had cleared we reversed the pump and grey, turgid glue poured into the dark-brown pool. We sprinkled it with several trowelfuls of *Chloriklar comprimés dissolution rapide* and went into the house before it could bite us.

We were both out the following morning at 5.30 a.m. and found we had a shimmering, golden pool – but solid gold, sufficiently opaque to obscure whatever marine life might still be lurking or even breeding on the bottom.

Madame let the skimmer have half a bottle of pay-ash minoos. Nothing happened for a moment and then an enormous bubble, like a geyser, burst out of the skimmer, and another and another and another. It was as though the filter plant hated pay-ash minoos and was battling in a frenzy to get rid of it. After about an hour the filter gave up, apparently having decided to take its pay-ash minoos like a man.

We back-washed. Green tar burst from the hosepipe. After it had cleared we reversed the pump and green tar gushed out into the pool.

We have now got back to where we started, with a kind of light, emerald pool. We have also run out of pay-ash minoos, and are thinking of starting on the ploos.

For myself, I wouldn't mind having six sturdy lads from the unhappily defunct Great Northern Railway, with railway lines and wheels, to see what they could do.

Not that they, with all their mighty valves and sleepers, could be of the slightest assistance to this – apparently – mad old man, sitting in a cane chair in the now empty shallow end of the pool, his describably filthy corduroy trousers rolled above the bare feet, under a tartan golf umbrella to shield him from the drizzling April rain.

He's got an animal, or a machine, beside him, protected by a plastic sheet, from which pipes and tubes spring out with the profusion and diversity of snakes in a pit.

Even a certifiable egomaniac passing by, reflecting on the state of his bank balance, his sudden lack of regard for his wife, his hatred of her dog and the condition of his front teeth would surely be jerked out of this stupor of auto-hypnosis, to stop by the edge of the pool to call down to the poor old codger, 'What goes forward there, my good man?'

He'd get an answer, if he did. Most definitely, he'd get a reply. I'd begin by saying, like a Cabinet Minister under severe pressure during a television interview, 'Ah, yes, well, I'm glad you asked me that one.' Because I want to explain to somebody, anybody, even a deaf mute, what I'm doing sitting on a chair down this accursed hole, for the reason that I'm getting lonely, desperate, homicidal and I want a second party to share my sufferings before they shatter my mind into a small pile of broken glass.

I got down here, it feels like weeks ago, because I wanted to pump out the now stagnant pool, clean it and refill it with sparkling white water. This enterprise began, absolutely inevitably, with dead silence from the pool pump when I switched it on for the first time since last October. The normal five-day wait for the electrician, who gets the motor going within half an hour and leaves the scene immediately when he finds that whilst the pump is pumping, no water is coming out of the other end.

Pete cures this. He drives boats for a living and knows – or gives the impression that he knows – every conceivable thing about every piece of machinery aerial, nautical or ter-restrial. Despite the fact that he is installing a pool for himself he's good enough to tell me on the telephone, 'You're sucking air from somewhere – have a look round your filter plate.'

It takes me the rest of the day to find an accessory that might well be the filter plate. I remove it, clean the rust from the underside, put it back on, screw it down tight and lovely stagnant water comes rushing out of the other end of the hosepipe. A winner!

I spend the rest of the following week pumping the stagnant all over our own garden, because I know what will happen if I let it run down the road. It will invade the nest of new villas at the bottom of the hill. The residents will step out into their gardens and find that something has flooded them overnight. It will take them three minutes to divine the source and another two to get them outside our gate, shouting and cradling drowned geraniums in their arms.

By the time the pump stops pumping our garden is so sodden that some of the smaller trees seem to be on the verge of floating away. I get out the handy little portable pump, re-arrange all the hosepipes, plug in the flex and the pump whines away without pumping a single drop of water. I prime the pump with the hose from the mains, jumping into the empty shallow end to adjust the inlet pipe, out again to plug in the flex and turn off the tap and in again to find out why no drop of water will emerge at the other end.

Pete cures this, too, actually coming in person in the middle of the bulldozer digging the hole for his own pool. He has ten miles of black cable on a drum, looks at my pump and says, 'Is she three-phase?' I make no reply, not knowing the answer. 'Is she a puller or a pusher?' I'm in the same position as before. 'She's only a half-kilowatt,' Pete says. 'Let's have her in the pool.'

The sight of the pump in the shallow end, throbbing with electricity within an inch of water, turns me to stone. But Pete gets it going, pumping away in torrents. He advises me to keep an eye on the whole set-up, moving the pump inch by inch, and the inlet pipe, down towards the bottom of the pool, as the water gets lower. Then he hurries back to his own house, as he is awaiting the delivery of the machinery and the liners for his own.

That's how I got down there, on the cane chair, with my trousers rolled up, under the tartan umbrella, because of the rain, pushing the pump down inch by inch, waiting for electrocution at every move.

Actually, all this had one redeeming feature. Madame came running out of the house with the news, 'Pete's pool's been pinched!'

It seemed impossible, but indeed his machinery and liners had finished up, far removed from his grasp, in somebody else's garage in circumstances that defied belief.

Sitting on the chair at the shallow end it was a comfort to know that I was guarding ours, while pumping it out, guaranteeing myself, if I last that long, another twenty years in the same hell-hole.

Hedging hats

We were coming back from the village when, out of the corner of my eye, in avoiding six fat men on racing bicycles and a forty ton lorry full of gravel, I caught a glimpse of Super Hedge with somebody actually clipping it – a phenomenon seen for the first time in ten years.

This hedge – cypress, of course – is always perfectly rectangular, with an absolutely flat top, an achievement beyond reach with this particular type of fauna.

I'd always thought that whoever was running this Super Hedge must trim it every night, with a torch, so that people passing by next day will be enraged by the belief that the owner has hit upon, or invented, a kind of cypress that grows square and, when it has risen to the required height, simply stops and remains plank-flat on top till the end of its days.

But here now was the Super Hedge runner actually clipping it, in full view at eleven o'clock in the morning, and working – if you please – with offensive ostentation. A small, wiry man with a hat made, apparently, of twisted hay, skipping ballet-like along the wall of his filthy straight hedge, giving it the final, miniscule snips on the way to the masterpiece, like some awful expensive Hollywood hairdresser doing repairs to Raquel Welch.

When I saw our hedge, with curiously new eyes, I became angrier with him than ever because our hedge, taking the rough with the smooth, the by with the large and making allowances in every direction, looked not so much like a rectangular, flat-topped cypress hedge as a squalid lump of vegetation in the middle of the Matto Grosso, rejected even for firewood by the local Indians.

Admittedly, I had been meaning to get round to it for some time. During this period, however, the hedge – about one hundred and fifty yards of it – had out of spite become veritable nest of weeds, the more vigorous of which had burst through the top of it, reaching for the sky.

We had that long, sticky weed that grows six feet a night from a cat's cradle of wiry yellow roots, competing with brambles that seemed on the verge of bursting into edible fruit, so buoyant was their health even at this fairly early season in the year. We had towering yellow stalks that looked like wild wheat, but they were towered over by stuff resembling even wilder peas. From the interstices of the rocks that border the road outside our cypress hedge sprang clump after clump of that nauseating growth with brown stalks and greenish-blue leaves that rises to the height of several feet, and once it's in it's there until nuclear war.

I was surprised to see what had happened to our hedge in so short a space of time. Probably due, I thought, to some abnormality in the weather, but equally possible thanks to some furtive weed seed strewing, in the middle of the night, by some envious competitor – and I didn't have to go farther than the hedge hairdresser in the hay hat to be able to identify *him*.

But what to do about it, now? The magnitude of the task was so obviously gigantic that nothing would be achieved by rushing at it like a bull, armed with slashers and hackers and machetes, knives and forks and trowels, pick-axes, shears and screwdrivers – all the fearful armament in my weed-fighting quiver. Some preliminary thought was required, even some knowledge lodged of the life and times of the cypress tree and the threats to its continued existence.

I turned to a gardening book. Of all the lunatic measures! I never look at gardening books because all gardening books, right there on Page One, begin to sound the toll that precedes, so very, very briefly, death. Unless you've mulched it, chalked it, nitrogened it, peated it, manured it and then protected it hermetically against rats, cats, dogs, babies, worms, earwigs and eels, whatever you may have planted is going to die, brother die, right there before your very eyes, and more quickly than you can possibly imagine.

The gardening book got off to a good start with CYPRESS. It said, 'See CUPRESS'. Of all the fantastic wastes of time—

I found CUPRESS. And stopped, instantly, up to the waist in contorted drivel. There is a kind of cypress called Cupressus Lawsoniana, but does Lawson, whoever he was, get a look in? There's another one called Chamaecyparis nootkatensis, but who's the criminal Esquimo called Nootkat? Some of them are glaucous, some are fastigiate, which is probably how they feel about the glauci, but there was nothing about – I stopped, suddenly, the lower jaw upon the breastbone. It said, 'Cones are 1-sexed. The males have 4–8 whorls of scales bearing clusters of stamens on the upper surface. They are small and fall off soon after maturity.'

Poor gentleman cones. Then I got a blow straight between the eyes. 'Female cones have few scales with ovules borne on the upper surface which on ripening become dry and weedy, or fleshy and berry-like.'

Under these circumstances I felt almost indelicate as I propped our tottery tin ladder against the fleshy and berry-like female cones and mounted it, keeping well to the left of the rungs because the right-hand side is weak.

In my free hand I carried the shears.

215

Against the heat of the sun I wore my faded pink raffia hat, turned up in front, and as my head rose above the top of the hedge one of two old ladies, after a small start at the unexpected apparition, said, *'Bonjour, Madame.'*

Two silly old things meandering along the lane, barely able to see where they were going, but having a nice little outing and wishing to be pleasant to all and sundry.

I will allow, at this point, that my hat had come from the ladies' millinery section of the *Supermarché*, like they all have for years, but I was sweating and purple in the face and unmistakably – I would have thought – all boy.

Before I could point this out, verbally, the ladder gave a lurch and I had to grab the hedge to save myself.

'Tiens!' the other old lady cried. *'Attention, Madame! Prenez garde!'*

I'd got the shears stuck in the top of my shorts and struggled to release them.

This predicament was invisible to the two old ladies but their concern remained undiminished.

The first one said, *'Mais, Madame, ça c'est trop difficile pour vous—'*

The second one cried, *'Allez chercher, Madame, votre mari.'*

I had to do something to stop this nonsense, but what? Some sense of personal dignity prevented me from looking down upon the two old women, wearing as I was a lady's hat, and saying in what was almost bound to be an over-declamatory style, '*Moi, je suis mâle.*'

There was another problem about this possible announcement. A Frenchman, or even an old French woman, in pronouncing the word '*mâle*' would probably be able to indicate the presence of the circumflex accent, and the final 'e'. If, however, I were to convey the news that I was '*mâle*' it would certainly come out as '*mal*'. So there I would be, wearing this lady's hat, looking down upon two old women from the top of a hedge, saying, 'I, I am sick', not, 'I, I am male'.

All this complex ratiocination takes time, of course, to describe, but in fact I went through it in a flash, even reaching the decision, with time to spare, that I wasn't going to tell them I was unwell. They would be in through the gate in no time and the jig would be up. I was wondering, hurriedly, what jig could be up, when I suddenly thought I could say, with stern composure, '*Moi, je suis un homme. Je m'appelle M'sieu Patrick Campbell*', emphasizing firmly the unquestionably masculine christian name. Or would it come out as, '*Patrice*'? Would, '*M'sieu Patrice*' make things even worse? '*Bonjour, Madame la transvestite—*'

The three of us continued to look at one another, with time passing rather more slowly for them than for me. In fact, they seemed to be engaged in some kind of discussion,

217

glancing up at the face above them, wearing this lady's hat.

Then the first one, a little doubtfully, said, '*Vous êtes peut-être Madame Tarragoni?*'

The other one said, '*Moi, je connais bien sa belle-soeur.*'

If I made a move in the sensible direction – i.e. downwards and out of sight – I knew the ladder would give way and there'd be a frightful clattering crash, shears embedded in the giblets, and the two old women bending over me a second later. On the other hand, I was not prepared to point out that I was not our own daily help but her employer, wearing a lady's hat. I continued to stare down at them, red-faced and sweating, devoid of speech, thought and hope. Then the first old woman said to the second one, in what she might have intended to be an inaudible aside, '*Mais, non – elle est trop âgée.*'

That did it. The suggestion that I couldn't be Madame Tarragoni because I was too old finally boiled my blood.

I seized the hedge and mounted to the top rung of the ladder, appearing bare chested like Aphrodite – no, Neptune – out of the foam.

The two old women clapped their hands to their eyes. The first one cried, '*Dégoûtant!*' The second one snapped, '*Quelle horreur!*' They set off at a sharp pace down the road.

Ever since then, I've been looking for a butch, masculine hat, as a guard against the torrid, if infrequent, Mediterranean sun.

Something just a little out of the ordinary. Certainly not one of those dreadful narrow-brimmed straw things, down in the front and up at the back, that so many holiday makers return to Luton in. Definitely not a cap and absolutely certainly not a hot-water bottle cover in sky-blue towelling. A Maurice Chevalier boater? A silk handkerchief in pastel shades knotted at the corners? I can tell you I was getting desperate – until I saw an advertisement in a year-old copy of the *New Yorker* magazine. And there it was! THE hat.

It was called the 'Eddie Bauer Derringer'. Weight 2¼ ozs. Colour: Straw Gold. Band: Genuine Apache/Pawnee/Blackfoot design (state preference). Shape: Authentic Stetson upward roll, to keep the sun out of your eyes and the rain off your glasses. Send only $11.95.

It was THE hat, all right. Looked lovely in the picture and Eddie Bauer himself said it was 'highly recommended for Western Dudes and sportsmen everywhere – will boost your morale and float you through summer's heat and humidity'. But the magazine was a year old, and Eddie Bauer's emporium was in Seattle, Washington 98124, USA. Perhaps he'd gone out of business? Or the Derringer had been discontinued?

In a fever of impatience and anxiety I wrote, express, to Sandy and Gregg, in Maine, imploring them to flash, instantly,

$11.95 to Ed, and get him to shovel the goods down here.

I waited for two weeks, biting my nails and anything else that came to hand. I hadn't had my hair cut for three months so I was worried about the head size. And also, mad-cap, impatient fool that I was, I'd forgotten to stipulate a Pawnee, as opposed to an Apache or Blackfoot, band.

A very large, rather battered, cardboard box arrived here on Wednesday, having been in transit for only five days from Seattle. I opened the box and took out my new Derringer.

It appeared to be made of some substance like very thin, iron-hard dog-biscuit, with a straw-gold sheen. The band was brown, black, white and red, either Apache, Pawnee or Blackfoot or, perhaps, a tribal merger of all three. Due, no doubt, to some bashing in transit, the Stetson upward roll was considerably more marked on one side than on the other. Looking at myself steadily in the mirror, I put it on.

A long, deeply melancholy face looked back. On top of it, well above the ears, stood a hard, dog-biscuit pot, flanked by upward flaring wings but one flaring more than the other, so that it seemed that either the Derringer, or the face, had been put on crooked.

I took if off and bent the high side down, very gently. It sprang back, with an audible report. On the hat-band, inside, it said, 'Self

Conforming'. 'You can say that again, cow-boy,' I said to myself, as bitterly as anything. Then I saw there was something else in the box. A catalogue. And what a catalogue. It revealed that Straw-Gold Derringers for Western Dudes were but a fraction of Eddie Bauer's stock in trade.

Ed, in fact, was mostly in goose down. There were hundreds of pictures of healthy, pioneer Americans wrapped in goose down literally from head to foot. There were goose down Mt. Everest bootees, goose down insulated suburban sports parkas, reversible hunter's vests, watch caps, goose down back-packer sweaters, chest protectors, muffs, hoods and dickeys, all in goose down, in-cluding a mask to cover the entire face save for two holes for the eyes. Around Eddie Bauer there couldn't have been a goose alive for hundreds of miles.

Nor was that all. We had sixteen-inch Snake Boots, Fishawk boots, amphibious flotation jackets, co-ordinated dress slacks, men's gaberdine westerns, stag shirt-jacs, all sports warm-up suits, waffle-weave thermal underwear and a sure-shot goose call in select black walnut expertly tuned to call Canadian Honkers. Plus, of course, my own Straw-Gold, super lightweight Derringer with the authentic Stetson roll, worn by Western Dudes and sportsmen everywhere.

I put it on again. And came to a number of conclusions.

If I was going to make the cap, as it were, fit, so that I could wear it, I was going to have to have my head shaved to the bone. Then, to firm the melancholy Irish face into something more backwoodsmanlike, a Pancho Villa moustache. Plus a Stag Shirt-Jacket or a Double Mackinaw Cruiser, a pair of Bedford Cord Westerns, a Hand-tooled Trophy Belt, Sperry Top Sider Over-Sock Boots and, finally, of course, a horse.

Except that at the moment, thanks be to God, Eddie Bauer didn't seem to be in that line of business.

Tin leaves and toads

Against all conceivable possibility they – both of them, by the sound of it – were not only awake – 5.32 a.m.! – but up and around and trying to get out.

I stood there, with the tools of my trade, and listened to the mess they were making of the hooked bar which so ingeniously keeps the shutters shut. They must have been awake for some time – long enough, at all events, to give her voice a distinct edge as she urged him to 'Open the damn thing or leave it alone.' He replied in very similar terms.

Obviously, they were nervous, as well they might be. Dropped in the previous evening, generously enough to deliver a parcel of books ordered in London, on their way to St Tropez, left their motor in molten sunshine and failed to start it upon attempted departure. Petrol all vaporized into steam. Endless whirring of starter, both of them leaning forward, faces almost against the windscreen, eager to be gone.

Just before he drained all the power from his battery I asked them to stay the night, despite Madame's presence on the balcony above. During the whirring business I had seen her yawn twice, serious cavernous stuff, white of eye only showing, the work of a lady already, at 7.20 p.m., two-thirds of the way into bed, and in the interest of speed more than ready to forego dinner.

She made dinner and we had some chat about the problems of gardening, during the heat wave, in Peebles, their base. We slotted them into the pool house by 11 p.m. – there was quite a lot about clay soil in Peebles – and ran up the stairs, shoulder to shoulder, each trying to get into our own basket first.

Now I waited for him or, more probably, her to master the intricacies of the hooked bar, and to emerge into the golden sunshine of the dawn.

It was clear that they had not perceived the trick of pulling the shutter inwards, to release the pressure of the hook in the eye-bolt.

223

'Morning!' I cried. 'Pull the shutter inwards to release the pressure of the hook in the eyebolt!'

I've perfected a very good hearty vicar's 'Morning!', all full of Rugger, cold baths and good works. I can tell you it's caused many a slugabed to jump out of his bedroom slippers, when it catches him unawares.

My merry bellow created instant and absolute silence. 'After,' I bawled, 'you have removed the hook from the eyebolt feed the bar into the vertical position by hand. If you let her swing she'll break the second window-pane from the bottom.'

It took them a surprisingly long time to work out these simple instructions. The shutters opened. They peered out.

'Morning!'

He started, and stood on her foot. They were both fully dressed and carrying their luggage.

'Oh,' he said. 'There you are.' And stopped. I was carrying a breathless Mrs Toad in one hand, my yellow bucket, yellow dustpan, broom and net in the other.

The two of them looked at the toad, and blinked. I explained. 'She falls into the pool every night, makes her way into the skimmer and waits for me to pick her out.'

They digested this uneasily. 'We,' she said in the end, 'We heard – noises.' He added to this. 'Sort of scratchy, crackling noises.' 'We thought,' she said, 'it might be a fire.' 'A forest fire,' he said, looking at the prettily flowering rockery.

'That was only me,' I said, 'brushing up tin olive leaves. At this time of year the leaves that fall are bone dry – just like tin, really – and if you get the concave side down the edges cling like billyoh to the terrace and it's the devil's own job to shift 'em with the brush.' (The healthy Vicar was in full cry this morning.)

'But,' he said, for some reason objecting to this full, clear explanation, 'there was a kind of scratching sound—'

'That was me, scuffling the boule court.' I tried to make it simpler. 'There's a lot of very fine sand on the boule court and when the tin leaves get mixed up in it you've got to take y'rake to it. Followed, of course, by cross-hatching with the broom to provide a smooth surface for subsequent play.'

They had the appearance of people being addressed in the dialect of one of the outer Japanese islands. She decided to defend herself. 'But,' she said, 'there was also a thin, screaming noise, like a dynamo and water, splashing about.'

'That was the automatic sprinkler. I turn it on first thing every morning, because the pressure dies out in the evening. Perhaps,' I suggested, 'you have the same thing in Peebles?'

The mention of the heartland gave him some kind of resolution. 'Well,' he said, 'we must be pushing – er – on.'

From the balcony, I watched them getting into their car. They didn't see me, above them. 'Tin olive leaves,' he said to her. 'That *toad*,' she said. 'And *scuffling* the boule court.' He said, 'Mad,' with surprising venom.

Mercifully, their car started immediately, and they drove away without further demonstration.

A streetcar named August

Do you know what you are, August?

I'm going to be absolutely frank with you, August. You, August, are a soppy, weepy, bedraggled old harridan. There, I've said it. Clearly, definitely, finally – and frankly.

Of all the months in the year you are beyond any possible question the most tedious, irritating, niggling, nagging, unstable, unreliable, unattractive – August, you're a mess.

I suddenly know what you are, August. You're the Blanche Dubois of the year. You came straight out of a *Streetcar Named Desire*. Faded glories, pitiful moments of defiance, flashes of beauty, followed by total wispy, weepy, *soppy* collapse.

It isn't often I turn against a month as passionately as this. Filthy February, of course, has had its comeuppance from time to time. Revolting November's had a belt of two around the ear. Disgusting December has not, on occasion, got off too lightly either. But at least you can say this much for those three ghastly months. They can't help it. They have no pretensions. They're stuck with being dank and dark and nauseating. They make no bones about it. Unlike August, who makes bones about everything, whatever the hell 'making bones' means.

August, you have worn out our cushions. You have not only worn out ten small cushions, six large ones, two mattresses and a couple of bolsters. You have worn me out as well.

Every evening, since you began, at a time of year when the whole world is on holiday – you could say at the very topmost, highest possible holiday season of the year – every evening, from God knows where, you've dredged up some clouds. Nothing to speak of, to begin with. Clouds no bigger than a woman's hand. Three times out of five I cannot believe you're going to do it again, and I leave the ten small cushions, the six large ones, the two mattresses and the couple of bolsters out, beside the pool, and then no sooner am I tucked up in basket with my rubber bone and down it comes. Drenching torrents of rain, at the absolute peak of the holiday season, when millions of innocent holiday makers are looking forward to paddling and ice-cream.

You're awful, August.

Quite often, in the evening, you don't dredge up any clouds at all. The summer moon rises, luminous and sweet. That's when I decide to put all the soft upholstery in the potting shed, because I don't trust you, you unspeakable jade, a single inch. I think again, because all this soft upholstery shovelling takes twenty-five minutes and when, finally, I add the two mattresses to the heap, propped up against my work bench, I've got to lean against the door before I can shut it.

So I think – well, look at that lovely luminous, cloudless moon, it can't possibly happen again – and I leave all this battered, tattered soft upholstery out and down she comes. Torrents, stair-rods, iron bars of rain. And not always in the evening, either.

Some mornings you begin as fair as fair. Soft blue skies and a grateful heat. I plunge like a lion into the potting shed, drag out the two mattresses, set them up on the two tin beds, cover tenderly with the blue towelling, add the two bolsters, lay out the ten small cushions and the six large ones and then it starts to rain.

I stand there, beside the pool, at the very peak of the holiday season, and I cannot believe it. Perhaps these are liver spots before my eyes, not rain. But you know, August, and I know, August, these are no liver spots. These are stair-rods, all over again. Soaked to the skin, twenty-five minutes later, I am leaning against the door of the potting shed, slamming it upon the sodden upholstery within.

For God's sake, have a heart. Without doubt, after the most wonderful summer in living memory, we are in for the worst winter the world has ever seen. Once you're over, August, it's going to be the end of the good old days. Millions of people returning to non-existent jobs, murder, arson, pillage and rapine. Portuguese golf-courses ploughed up to plant vegetables, the bottom falling out of the Suez Canal, the Chinese going all nuclear and another draconian British budget once every three days. And all you can do is to rain, and on occasion out of a clear blue sky, at that, so that I'm stuck half in and half out of the potting shed with six small cushions on my head and a mattress under either arm.

Suddenly, I realize that it's later than I think. Today is surely thirty-first of August? Tomorrow is the beginning of September. Autumn. Falling leaves. Mud. Cold. The month in which the drains get blocked and the world wars begin . . .

August, darling August, come back! I didn't mean it. I promise you. I was mad, drunk, sick, only joking.

Come back, beautiful, gentle, lovely

August, and never leave us again. We *need* you.

You're about the only thing, rain or shine, that separates us from the horrors of Christmas.

Gangrene in the violets

Having had the wettest summer ever known on the Côte d'Azur we are now having the filthiest spring. Unshiftable, armour-plated grey skies, lashing, bitter rain, even thunderstorms, with fierce bright-green lightning to give, at least, a touch of colour to the sodden scene.

Nonetheless – and that, to me, is a substantial nonetheless – the serious gardeners are beginning to stir from their winter lairs, heavy footed in rubber boots, almost tubular in woollies, any old hat crushed down about their ears, to look with deep reflection upon the rubbish left over from last year, oblivious to the meteorological fact that while, at the moment, it isn't raining it will, in the next twenty minutes, start belting down all over again.

I know what this deeply reflective look portends. It means that all that leggy lavender will be torn out, by the ton. The previously neat but now flea-bitten rosemary hedges will go to join the lavender on the bonfire, with something like £50 worth of *Thuya orientalis Aurea Nana* bushes piled high on top, all this wholesale destruction preceding a whole new design, which should have been there in the first place, years ago.

Inside the house, of course, beside the comforts of the fire, we have gardens, superbly healthy, blazing away in all the colours of the rainbow, impervious to the revolting weather outside. They are in the new gardening books, in full colour, which fall upon us at this season of the year with the persistency of hail. Mercifully, in place of a cash transaction, they have been borrowed from people who are still friends, and might continue to be if they get them back.

It was from a laggardly browsing through one of these volumes that I got to know *Thuya orientalis Aurea Nana*, which might possibly be a bush but sounds much more like a phosphorescent Chinese banana. Next, I came upon a *Sequoia sempervirens Prostrata*, surely an elderly Red Indian chief who's going to live nearly for ever if he has an urgent operation. Finding myself becoming, perhaps, over-trivial in this study of scientific gardening, I turned several lumps of heavy pages in search of a new theme and ran, without warning, into a veritable charnel house of plague and disease, a list of afflictions so appalling that, in human beings, smallpox and a touch of rabies on the side became no more threatening than a slight cold in the head.

I've never heard such dread news in my life. The author, Doctor – I mean, Mr – S. Millar Gault, giving not a fig – *Ficus carica* -- for the bedside manner, started us off in the operating theatre, already covered in blood. Lecturing as he slices he tells us to preserve good garden hygiene by removing all dead, damaged or diseased growths of leaves, cleaning up any wounds with a sharp knife or chisel and treat with a paint dressing or preferably bituminous, asphalt compound. A slaughterhouse. Imagine attacking, say, a *Filipendula* with hammer and chisel, lopping off the pendula bit, and slapping a shovelful of tarry asphalt all over anything that's left.

And yet, in the operating theatre, things are relatively straightforward. Get out into the public wards and see what's possible in the way of pustulence, gangrene, rot and decay.

Acer Scorch, for instance, turns you brown around the edges, followed by curling and shrivelling, with the good news to follow that nothing can be done. If you've got Clematis Wilt you suddenly droop from the top downwards and, for your trouble, get sprayed with dithiocarbamate fungicide every two weeks. Coral Spot is fun, known to Doctor as *Lectria cinnabarina*. It's only pink or red cushions like pustules, probably appearing on the end of the nose.

A limitless history of disaster. You can get Fire Blight, the treatment of which begins by having it reported to the Government, after which you get grubbed out and destroyed. Honey Fungus, better known to the coarser nurses as 'bootlaces', often finishes you off before you even know you've got it. Pyracantha Scab, Rhododendron Bud Blast and – for Heaven's sake – Azalea Gall, reddish small plums appearing on the leaves, which Americans *eat*, calling them Pinxterapples, and sometimes survive, the first good news we've had in weeks.

But I've got some even gladder tidings for gardeners everywhere. Solve all your problems by getting lots and lots of bituminous apshalt, spread it evenly all over your grounds and stand back, sneering, watching Rhododendron Bud Blast trying to blow its way out of that.

Auntie tree

I think that I shall never see
A hole as sad as in which once
There stood a flowery tree.

Second line perhaps a little rough, grammatically, but the tree got rough justice, too.

An orange tree that had lived for perhaps eighty years in the little courtyard in front of the house. We used it as a Christmas tree, hanging parcels among the oranges which, to our earlier surprise, became round and ripe in the middle of the winter.

At some time the tree had suffered a fearful blow – lightning, an axe, arthritis? – that had divided the trunk in two, a shock that caused it to produce seedless fruit on one side and stuff bulging with pips on the other.

The other shock it got was when, six years ago, we had heavy snow in March, against all conceivable probability, and it became leafless, stone bald, taking three years to recover, but only just. It was round about then that she turned into a woman. Our expert olive tree trimmer, looking at it with compassion, said, 'She's getting to be a very old lady.'

I do not exaggerate when I say that the eyes – two each – of Madame and me filled with tears. Nor do I err when I aver – that opening gust of poetry clings to me like ivy – when I aver that from then on Madame treated that tree like a beloved old aunt.

Treated is the very word. No medicament was too costly. The division in the trunk was tenderly coated with mastic. The leaves were sprayed, even washed – thousands of them – by hand. This spring she was laden with snow-white blossom and then, suddenly, everything – leaves and blossom and tiny, embryo oranges – began to fall off.

'Chop her down,' said Headmaster (rtd) Bayliss lunching with us in her shade, his plate filled with débris. Madame choked back a sob, and a mouthful of leaves. 'Do it now,' she said. In fifteen minutes the three of us had reduced eighty years' of growth to a stump, with the dismembered limbs of the old lady on the rubbish dump. (By gum, poetry *again*!)

A young man built like Mohammad Ali, but paler, came and hacked out the stump, severing roots as thick as his own leg. He refilled the hole like lightning, tiled it over to match the rest of the courtyard and left us to an inferno.

About a quarter of this courtyard is shaded by a tunnel of vines. The rest of it was shaded by the orange tree. Without the tree we were like two sausages sitting side by side on cane chairs in a huge frying pan.

The powerful young man came back again and in a day increased the width of the tunnel with iron bars and wire, beating the standing record of eight months for the construction of the original – i.e. six months waiting for the bars and the wire and two months for their erection.

Madame, feverishly wiping out the memory of the murder of her beloved old auntie, began to refurnish the courtyard. We got rid of the small rectangular table and brought up the large, round teak. After that she wanted a large, round weatherproof tablecloth and, as an aesthetic afterthought, four matching cushions for the metal dining chairs and, by a further rational progression, six new cane chairs as the old ones looked so shabby, or would when she found the new tablecloth. And, while we were at it, we were certainly in need of three new umbrellas, to replace the five-year-old existing ones which she found were disfiguring the pool.

I pointed out that total bankruptcy might be excessive punishment for the cutting down of a tree. She replied by getting hold of Pippa and her station wagon and speeding off to sack the city of Nice, knowing that I, personally, would be as ready to drive to Nice in the summer as I would be to venture into Beyrouth, under its present circumstances.

In addition to the mountain of treasure with which they returned they also had six beach mattresses of thin straw – for me to roof the addition to the vine tunnel, on the grounds that the vines might not grow sufficiently quickly to provide shade for the new tablecloth. They also had some linen thread, with which I could sew the mattresses to the wires.

It took me the whole of the afternoon, but it looked pretty good when I'd done it. Next morning, at 5.25, when the wind sprang up, it looked like a square-rigged clipper ship in a full gale off Cape Horn.

As I stood, for hours, on top of the ladder, holding the writhing mattresses down with my elbows, trying to stuff the lumpy linen thread through the eye of the needle and save the ship in the nick of time, I reflected that whilst the tree might have been looking at God all day no one had been listening when she lifted her leafy arms to pray.

And, by God, more was the pity.

Chairs in Concrete

The geniuses who thought of, and made, garden furniture, some of it in Grade B tin, must surely have had rain in mind as one of their major technical problems.

'Right, then,' they must have said, 'what we want to do is to get armchairs, smallish sofas, eating tables, coffee tables and – well – dining-room chairs out of the house and into the garden, car-park or lay-by. Right? Well, then, it would be pretty barmy to have all this stuff made of walnut-type veneer, on a base of orange boxes, or cover y'chairs with off-maroon moquette, on the lines of the junk we've got inside. No. We've got to rejig our thinking. We've got to slip the customer something that will be approximately the same shape and colour, after a couple of days of average heavy summer rain, as what it was when they took delivery of same. Right? But here's another point. If they haven't got the wit or the speed to cover it with a sheet of plastic or Auntie's second best mac *before* the rain comes belting down let's give 'em something they can fold up in a trice and bung into the potting shed or, alternatively, a piece of furniture so heavy – a Chippendale style imitation teak *chaise longue* – that they couldn't shift it with a crane . . .'

It may seem uncharitable thus to speculate upon the deliberations of garden furniture manufacturers the world over until, that is, one comes to examine with even minimal care the nature of the goods they provide.

Take the deck chair. Well and good, certainly, on the deck of a ship, in that they can be folded up and put away so that the matelots can get on with their swabbin' down, but a deck chair in a garden is like sitting in a prepared mouse-trap, ready to snap at the slightest movement of an incumbent posterior. Not that they don't do the same thing on boats.

Madame, daughter Brigid and I remember, with pleasure, watching two elderly English ladies, of archaeological disposition, setting up a couple of deck chairs preparatory to entering, on a small Greek packet, the Corinth Canal. The obvious leader was called Madge, the other one merely 'Dear'. Well, 'Dear', with one leg through the crosspiece of her deck chair, very nearly got it on until Madge came to her aid, only to get her cardie caught in the notches of hers. In the ensuing struggle Madge actually managed to get her canvas over 'Dear's' head, so they had a right old rumble-tumble, whilst we restrained ourselves as best we could.

Afloat or ashore, never trust a deck chair. The screeching split of canvas and the sudden descent upon the gaping jaws of one's own rum punch, lurking in the shade below. Too painful for words.

This drenching summer on the Côte d'Azur has dissolved our cane chairs as though they had been formed from blotting paper, leaving canes sprouting out like the spokes of a ruptured bicycle, armed with rusty nails. Seeking to replace them, after several years of vigorous sitting, we found that the price, for exactly the same commodity, had mounted itself from forty francs to one hundred and eighty-five, exclusive as ever of the price of the cushion, once retailing at fifteen francs and now fifty-nine. Nor was the cushion available in the old, simple true-blue. Now it came in livid green, dotted with a Paisley acne in ginger, mauve and puce.

We had a look at wooden-slatted garden furniture, at about the same price, made – we suspected – of hardboard painted white, with the slats on the tables so far apart that a bottle of Château Lafitte could have slipped through without touching the sides. The chairs were like sitting on a steel device for catching the hooves of cows.

From there we moved into plastic *al fresco* furnishings, moulded in the manner of Byzantine Jacobean, with undertones of Queen Anne. Some of the suites were gleaming white but others, having been in the shop too long, had matured to a dingy grey. A furtive rub with a handkerchief made no difference of any kind.

In search of a more durable product we entered an establishment so luxurious in *ambience* that we quickly found we were the only people there, apart from a surprised young man who appeared to be in charge. What surprised him was the fact that we, wearing no noticeable furs of jewellery, had come in at all, in view of the fact that one of his ordinary chairs, in lacquered aluminium, was going at the equivalent of £175, admittedly with a couple of cushions thrown in. I tried it for size and, at £175, found it a little cramped, seeing that we really need eight: i.e. £1,400 worth of garden sitting, trying to get our money's worth all day long in heavy rain.

Madame has now had a sensible idea. Moulded concrete furniture, scattered with home-made cushions, there indestructibly for ever, right there where it's been made.

At least no one's going to pull up *his* chair, confidentially to my side.

A procession of caterpillars

If it hadn't been for this grey, furry hat apparently stuck to one of the thin, upper branches of the sickly looking pine I would not have been compelled, with any luck, to return to the subject of gardening for quite some time.

This hat-like thing, however, engaged my attention on sight, exuding – as it did – an almost supernatural aura. Connections with ectoplasm, the lair of some small but malevolent monster, something nasty to do with witches – this fat, chunky, hairy-furry object seemed to come directly from what I thought of as the Other Side.

Fortunately, it was not in our garden, but in the garden of the house which Tom and Elise have recently rented on the other side of the road. We haven't got a pine tree, but if we had had one I would, at least, have had the satisfaction of watching, day by day, the activities of whoever, or whatever, was making it or even have had the good fortune to have been there, improbably enough at the witching hour of midnight, when it suddenly came plummeting down from the sky, and stuck.

It was only by chance that I found out what was in it. By Tom's request, and in his temporary absence, I was showing our own hired hedge and tree clipper around Tom's garden, it being, after long neglect, in urgent need of a short back and sides. The tree clipper started violently when he saw the furry hat. '*Oo-la!*' he cried. And when a big, powerful Frenchman says '*Oo-la!*' it doesn't sound in the least like the 'Oo-la-la' even of veteran Can-Can dancers. It sounds like the voice of doom.

And doom it was. The object was a nest of insects called aphis and must be destroyed at once before they got out of their hat and munched the whole of the neglected garden down to the ground. Unfortunately, he himself was much occupied at the moment and would not be able to attend to the

242

extermination of the hat for several weeks. On this disturbing note, he left.

In the continuing absence of Tom and Elise I worked out a plan for the immediate rescue of their garden. Say, if I got a long bamboo pole, wrapped a heavy dishcloth around one end, soaked it in paraffin oil, touched a match to it and hoisted this torch to the hat, frying it and its inhabitants alive?

A number of *contras* established themselves as quickly as the idea. The hat might explode. The whole pine tree could go on fire. The hat, burning fiercely, might drop straight down on top of my head, shooting a cascade of grilled aphis down the back of my neck, to be halted only by the inner soles of my boots.

I decided to wait until Tom came home, so that we could work out a more practical method, like he himself holding the pole.

In this difficult matter, chance took a hand again. Hiram, a world heavyweight in the field of horticulture, happened to be on the telephone about something else, so that I was able to slip in Tom's problem, round about the middle of it.

'Hiram,' I said, 'if you've got a grey, furry hat filled with aphis, what do you do about it?'

Hiram, ready for anything in a garden, said, 'Those aren't aphis. They're processional caterpillars. They come out of their hat at night, walk about in a long crocodile, eating and get back to bed before dawn. You can get them to walk in a circle, with a piece of stick, until they all die of hunger. It's quicker, of course, if you just chop the hat off the tree.'

I was round to Tom early the following morning, with the good news, only to find that the hat had been, as it were, lifted. Gone. Disappeared. Tom had amputated it by the most ingenious mechanism imaginable.

He had lassooed the top of the tree 'with a useful length of pinkish nylon rope', pulled the tree down into a half-circle, gave Elise the end of the rope to hold, chopped off the hat and burnt it, and that was the end of a neat morning's work.

My mind reeled. They were both lucky to have got it as neat as that. Say the tree had snapped in half, releasing the tension on the rope so unexpectedly that Elise had been whipped backwards through the bathroom window and straight into the bath. Or, perhaps, suspecting that the rope was going to do this, Elise had let it go, with the result that the tree had catapulted the hat clean over the road, on to the very head of an old lady next door.

It was maddening that I should have missed a potential as quivering as this.

And even more irritating that I'd been given no chance to turn a procession of caterpillars into an endless circle, with an instrument as simple as a piece of stick.

Pod lobbin'

This ought to be called pod lobbin' or – or bean spraddlin' – something with a crafty, rustic dignity to it. Not just a matter of tearing these fragile, giant, juicy stalks, laden with quite a lot of stuff resembling smallish, green bananas, with lumps, out of the ground, and tearing off the bananas and putting them into two blue plastic buckets, one red one and one yellow one and then throwing the stalks on to the bonfire that the law of Provence will not permit me to burn until late autumn, because they think if I do it now I will start forest conflagrations that will eventually consume costly properties like the Palm Beach Casino in Cannes and several retired British bookmakers on the terrace of the Carlton Hotel who, up till then, had been paying their bills like men . . .

You can see I'm pod lobbin', performing one of the mindless, repetitious and exquisitely tedious tasks that are the basis of gardening, liquifying at the same time any rational process of thought that might still be resident in the brain. Bean spraddlin' as I am, I cannot imagine how retired British bookmakers could possibly have entered my consciousness whilst being prepared, simultaneously, for even more ornately decorated junk to intervene.

Suddenly, bean spraddlin', I start back in fear, for I've just run into, dimly seen among its tiny brothers, the biggest pea-pod in the world. A pea-pod so big that it might well snap at, and consume, passing birds. The beans and the peas are contiguous. One single pea-pod has caught giantism off its neighbours and unless instantly slashed to death will turn the whole of Nature inside out. Then I see that it's really a bean that has, on a long, long juicy stalk, infiltrated the pea patch, so I tear it off and throw it fiercely, as punishment, into the yellow bucket, the mind all fluffy like angora wool.

It is with this fluffy mind that I seat myself, in my conical Thailand hat and my capacious Kensington shorts, in the little garden, because at long last the sun has arrived, having circumvented all those millions of Russian pine trees planted by wily Ivan to turn European weather back to front. Actually, I don't have a lot of time to think about this because I'm too busy arranging my buckets. Four buckets of still podded beans to the left, one empty bucket, for de-podded beans, between my legs and two more empty buckets, for de-beaned pods, on the right. All set and steady and ready to go.

The first bean, a veritable giant, shoots high in the air, under manual pressure, as though propelled by gunpowder, and plunges into the glass of beer with which I have equipped myself, even at this comparatively early hour, in case of the sitting staggers of any other malaise of a similar nature. I have invented a new drink, far more original than that boring old onion in the dry Martini! Eureka! What an exciting incident.

Nothing much happens during twenty-three more pods. I have found that if I tear the string off *both* sides of the bean one bean in seven comes apart most beautifully, so that it's a simple matter to nudge the contents into the relevant bucket. On the other hand the other six, de-stringed, cling to their pearls with redoubled determination and have to be torn apart as by a madman. And, oh boy, if only they were pearls.

But Pod twenty-four turns out to be a real swine. Probably the one that got into the pea-patch. Six lovely lumps on the pod and six miniscule brown dots inside. An hysterical pregnancy? Wind? Is there a doctor in the vegetable garden?

An hour later I have slid even further into mania. I have spraddled two buckets of pods and won a quarter of a bucket of beans. In leaving my chair to get another beaned beer I knocked over this bucket and had to replace every single one of them by hand. As a result I got beans on the brain. Awful man called Archie puts a banana-like finger along a bulbous nose and, nudge, nudge, says, 'Old

Charlie, God bless 'im, know how many beans make five.' Absolutely meaningless, infuriating one's very soul. Give 'im beans. At a bean-feast. While he's full of beans. Is there nothing else except beans in the whole wide world?

Three hours, less four minutes, after the commencement of pod lobbin', I have three-quarters of a bucket of de-podded beans and have carted away, to my amazement, no less than seven buckets of de-beaned pods. I was also taken aback by the number of beans that arrived from my capacious Kensington shorts when I stood up, seeing that I hadn't spotted them going in.

Madame deep-freezes my horde and we have the residue for lunch. I notice that the larger beans have smaller, greener beans inside their skin. I offer to peel her larger beans for her but she just looks at me steadily, without saying anything.

Beaned. With a beanpole.

Watering time, please

It is the bee-less hour of evening when flowers droop languidly in the breathless silence like diaphanous women dizzied by the heat of the day – that poignant moment when all Nature seems to pant, as the hart, for cooling streams and it's perfectly clear we're not going to get very much further in that vein so let me just say that blasted watering time has come round again and if I don't do it now the whole blithering garden's going to be stone dead by breakfast time, curse it, backwards and forwards and upside down.

Watering time brings on that kind of subtle reaction because as sure as hell after we've coupled up the hose to the tap on one side of the summer house and pulled the spout end round to water the golden erysipelas on the other some unseen obstruction is going to get in the way and we're going to give the hose a jerk that would break the neck of an ostrich and there will be a sudden crash and the sudden crash will be the new ornamental stone-type pot purchased at enormous cost that very day and newly planted with tufted trychinosis and the pot breaks into a million pieces and the syringe comes off the end of the hose and we get the lot all over our new sky-blue trousers. Curse it to hell and gone and back again.

It was to avoid that type of irritation that we had underground watering installed four or five years ago, with an electric pump to do the work. The garden, after being a jungle of brambles, thistles, Old Man's Bed Sock, Mother-in-Law's Snout and Virgin's Vertigo, was just beginning to look like a garden but the underground watering installers quickly took care of that. Twelve trenches two feet deep and twenty or thirty yards in length turned our lovesome thing into a scale model of the Somme, 1915, at the cost of an Austin 1100, 1969.

But it worked. I only had to lie full length in front of the small dog kennel – standard fitting – in which the pump had been installed, turn on four valves, press the switch and the whole place was bathed in leaping fountains – or was until I accidentally mowed one of the fountain heads concealed in the grass. From that source then arose a single gusher fifty feet high, while all the other points simply bubbled.

A man came to see about it, seven telephone calls, three letters and a telegram, reply pre-paid, later. He was bearded, French and his ankle was bandaged, having fallen into one of his own trenches some weeks before. Just as he began his work he gave me a keen glance and said, '*Evidemment, vous êtes an homme de Jésus, vous-même.*'

This was in the days when my French was rustier than it is now – i.e. total incomprehension even of a simple greeting, if delivered too abruptly – and I thought he suspected me of being a lay-preacher or part-time monk. A one-sided discourse of what I judged by its tone to be an excessive piety then took place, which he terminated by placing a hand on my head and murmuring some words which, for all I knew, might have turned me into a Roman Catholic.

Thus, when I switched on the underground watering system last week for the first time this year, and it failed to work, I came to an instant and irrevocable decision. Under no circumstances whatever would I send for help to the firm who had installed the system, just in case of you know what. Despite his habit of falling into his own trenches, lost no doubt in contemplation of matters spiritual, the bearded brother might well be still on the payroll and expecting me in the meanwhile to have risen to the eminence of Monsignor or, at the very least, Deputy Father Abbot.

I dismantled, cleaned and reassembled twenty-four sprays, learning their intricacies as I went along and putting quite a lot of them together the right way round first time. I pressed the switch and not a drop of water emerged from a single one. I got my head and shoulders into the dog kennel, with hatchet, screwdriver and hammer, found I had an airlock, dragged the hose to the rescue, breaking only one agrocarpis maxissima, primed the whole system with gallons of water, pressed the switch and – whoosh – off she went, fountain after fountain leaping in the evening aid.

Two of them got Jackie fore and aft, returning with previously dry clothes from the washing line. Four more nailed Charlie in his chair, placed to catch the westering sun. Another one did Madame's silk shirt, on her at the time and a fourth propelled the cat Spot from a supine position into the topmost branches of the cherry tree.

In the subsequent recriminations I learned that they had seen what I was trying to do but didn't think it would work.

They couldn't have known, of course, by what demons or, rather, angels, I was driven.

Fittipaldi's garden

Place the edge of the crescent-shaped blade just behind this mountainous yellow tuft of scutch grass, ensure that the big toe, protruding tenderly from its rubber sandal, is absolutely nowhere near the scene of operation, press down sharply on the handle of the blade, lever up the yellow tuft with its long green fronds, flick the whole consignment into the wheelbarrow and – lo – civilization has come to the jungle.

In place of an awful yellow tuft of scutch grass, with long green fronds, smothering the geraniums and allied vegetable, we now have a clean straight line.

What we do next is to place the edge of the crescent-shaped blade just behind the next mountainous yellow tuft of scutch grass, ensure that the big toe, etc., press down sharply, lever up in the prescribed manner, flick and – lo – civilization has advanced another step.

Our next action is to place the crescent-shaped whatsit behind the doodah, press, lever, flick it into the bleedin' barra, and on and on and on until the end of time.

I began this task ten days ago, wearing a gossamer weight, cone-shaped straw hat with a wide brim turned sharply up all round, purchased in Thailand last November, and I have still, by a quick visual estimate, another fortnight of pressing, levering and flicking before me.

Of course, pressing, levering and flicking are not the whole story. After these processes have taken place you've then got to do vertical trimming with the vertical, long-handled trimming shears *and after that* horizontal trimming with the long-handled horizontal trimmer, if civilization is to maintain its hold.

Sometimes exciting things happen. I can run into a buried stone, so that pressing is arrested almost immediately, until I've trowelled out the impediment. On other, fairly frequent, occasions, a branch tips my cone-shaped Thailand hat right over my eyes so that, until I've made the adjustment, I feel like a terrified Vietnamese virgin on the run from the Vietcong.

But mostly it's just pressing, levering and flicking, round the grass, round the flower-beds, round the trees, mile upon mile of it, day after day.

A senior executive in industry or commerce, writhing at his desk, making three wrong decisions out of every five in every hour, might suppose that a repetitive, purely physical task such as edging – or, indeed, any similar assembly line job – might lead to paralysis of the brain. Would that it did, senior executive, sir. In fact, repetitive, purely physical tasks such as edging bring about a leaping, coruscating, unceasing activity in that supposedly numb organ, so that one actually has to get off the assembly line to give it a rest before it boils, irretrievably, over.

All through last Monday morning, for instance, despite the cone-shaped Thailand hat and semi-bare feet, I was an old Suffolk (Norfolk) labourer, edgin' away like billyo.

'When March be owt,' I would mutter – *press*– 'edgin's abowt' – *lever* – 'bor' – *flick.*

It wasn't easy, as I've never heard either aged Norfolk – or Suffolk – edgers actually speaking about the job. Nor was I too certain about 'Bor'. What could it possibly mean? Boy? Brother? It didn't matter. I was stuck with it. 'When March be owt edgin's abowt, bor.' Perhaps one hundred and fifty times per barrow-load. I tried singing, *In a Little Spanish Town* – a deflector if ever there was one – and was back with bor in a matter of minutes.

Then a fearful thing happened. A friend of

254

mine wrote to me from Ireland to say that he'd been cutting down a very large fir tree and had got stuck with 'Emerson Fittipaldi'. He said he had no interest in motoring racing nor in the World's Champion driver but there he was stuck with 'Emerson Fittipaldi' in the midst of the Grand Prix scream of his motorized chain-saw. He went on to say the he'd hoped that 'Emerson Fittipaldi' would be confined to tree-cutting activities, but had been appalled to find that he'd got it again while disentangling his fishing line from a tree on the banks of the River Slaney. Except that it had now, for no known reason, become, '*T*. Emerson Fittipaldi'.

I got it at once, with knobs on. Over and over again, churning through the mind, while pressing, levering and flicking:

> *Fittipaldi – palsy-walsy,*
> *How does your garden grow?*

With a mental effort that would have left Einstein calling for oxygen I'd just got back to the old Norfolk edger when I read about the Spanish Grand Prix disaster, and Palsy-Walsy's refusal to take part in the race. And he's bound to be driving in the Monte Carlo Grand Prix in a few days' time.

What a fate. Fifteen miles of edging to go and Fittipaldi, palsy-walsy, on the brain.

Bean in a bassoon

After a night of howling wind, crashing branches and flying garden chairs summer seems to have broken out on the Côte d'Azur. The first true-blue sky in weeks and the sun hot on the pyjamas at six o'clock in the morning. Time to start running, and jumping, like a Mexican bean in a bassoon.

I wish I hadn't thought of a Mexican bean in a bassoon. I was really thinking of myself as a pea in a whistle – an object whirled around in an enclosed space by forces beyond its control, but it didn't seem to be big enough, so this image arrived of the bassooned bean. I really wish it hadn't because God knows I've got enough to do, now that summer has suddenly broken out, without having to worry about beans in bassoons. Like, is there a place in a bassoon to put a Mexican jumping bean so that when someone blows the bassoon he won't blow the bean out, depriving us of the picture of an object whirled around in an enclosed space by forces beyond . . .

I start running – first time since August, 1973 – to the shed at the very furthest end of the garden, wherein lies the pump with which I propose to pump out the million gallons of winter rainwater lying in the plastic cover over the pool at the same time spreading fertilizer on the clover, plaintains and dandelions that constitute our verdant lawns and watering it in with the water from the plastic cover because if I don't do it instantly the fertilizer burns the clover.

The running action dies out after perhaps twenty yards, but it begins again, instantly, when I find I've left the wheelbarrow at the end of the garden opposite to the pump-containing shed and I've suddenly remembered that if I don't transport the pump to the poolside in the wheelbarrow, but try to carry it instead, after a very few paces the whole garden begins to whirl round like a Mexican jumping bean in an enclosed . . .

All at once this lightning onset of summer has deprived me of time. At one moment there was all the time in the world, with the bitter north wind howling down from the Alps, the garden unapproachable and the oven clock grudgingly grungeing out the laggard hours. It did grunge. Something worn with its bearings. Deep, hopeless, groaning, grungeing, hour after hour, while keeping perfect time. Now we've got a new one and the seconds slip away silently, like lightning, like feathers in a hurricane – while grass grows in the long gravel path and all the edges of all the flower beds are as bearded as the pard and getting whiskerery by the minute and what in the name of all that's holy is a whiskerery pard? Cancel that. What is just a plain pard?

Running back with the wheelbarrow I wonder if other gardeners, suddenly faced with an unclimbable mountain of gardening, get their minds littered with jumping beans, grungeing clocks and bearded pards or whether they just wonder what to put the raffia around after they've mulched and before I've really got through that I'm back at the pool with the pump, couple up the hoses and throw the one with the heavy filter on it into the plastic cover and by gum it goes clean through it.

If I'd poised myself, like a javeling thrower, with the pitchfork, and flung it straight down through the plastic, it couldn't have made a bigger – or quicker – hole.

All the rubbish of winter, running like commuters for a train, rushes into the hole and disappears into the swimming-pool beneath. I scorch the dandelions on my own rush back to the shed at the furthest end of the garden to get the long-handled brush with which I normally sweep the bottom of the pool but with which I now intend to prevent any more muck falling through the hole. When I get back to the pool with the brush I switch on the pump – a split-second decision – because obviously, in the present emergency, the quicker I get the water out of the cover the better and I'm sweeping back the leaves like a madman when I realize that the exit end of the hose has sneaked itself in through the open door of the pool pavilion and is pumping muddy water all over the marble-type floor – and one white rug.

It's enough to bring on lunacy. Stemming the rushing leaves with the brush, held in the right hand, I snatch the hose out of the pavilion with the left and that looks after both trouser legs. Both boots are also filled before I can throw the malignant pumping end away.

I am aware that my good wife is standing beside me.

'What,' she says calmly, 'in the world are you doing? I've been watching you from the window and for the last ten minutes you've been whizzing around like a pea in a whistle.'

I didn't tell her about the jumping bean in the bassoon. I seemed to have enough on my plate already.

Adding it all up

I'd brought in two baskets of logs, thirty-eight in the first and thirty-four in the second, because in the second basket four – 1,2,3,4 – of the logs were larger than those in the first, and then I laid the lunch table, counting each utensil in this half-whispered way I do now and when the guests arrived I gave them drinks – 1,2,3,4,5 – and then I sat down with my own – 6 and counted this movement also, making 7.

They began to talk, some social nonsense about Christopher having left Helen for – you'll never believe it – Julian, but I couldn't wait any longer.

'You'll never believe this either,' I said, 'but five hundred olives weigh one-tenth of a kilogram.'

The response was immediate. 'No,' they cried, as 2 – 1,2 – men and 3 – 1,2,3 – women, 'not olives! We're sick of olives! Anything but olives—'

'Nine,' I said.

Someone said, 'Nine what?'

'Nine words,' I explained. 'Between the five – 1,2,3,4,5, – of you you've used nine – 1,2,3,4,5,6,7,8,9 – words.'

'What's this counting kick?' a woman wanted to know.

'If you'd been picking up olives, one by one, 6 – 1,2,3,4,5,6 – hours a day for the last three – 1,2,3 – months you'd be counting too,' I said. 'And to think it was only yesterday,' I went on, 'that I thought to find out how much five hundred olives weighed.'

A voice, on a declining note, said, 'Oh, God . . .'

'So,' I said, 'if five hundred olives weigh one-tenth of a kilogram that must be five thousand olives per kilo. Right?'

No one replied. Some were staring out of the window, others looking at the floor. There was a spiritless air about them, but I didn't mind.

'Now,' I said, 'you've got this wooden bucket, you see, which is called *une mesure*, and it contains two – 1,2, – décalitres of water, which is, of course, twenty litres – 1,2,3,4,—'

Someone moaned. It threw me out, not being allowed to count out loud up to twenty, but I went on, after a moment. 'The extraordinary thing is that twenty litres of water weigh twenty kilos, but twenty litres of olives weigh only twelve – 1,2,3,4,5,6 ahem – twelve kilos. It must be the air around the olives, because by this time, naturally enough, quite a lot of each olive has been munched by birds, leaving little holes into which the air can get.'

'What time is it?' someone said.

'This won't take more than three or four – 1,2,3, or 4 – minutes,' I said. 'It's fascinating. If we've got five thousand olives per kilo and there are twelve kilos per *mesure* that means that every *mesure* holds 60,000 olives. Approximately, of course, allowing for bird munching, wrinkling, shrinkage and so on.'

One of the girls said, 'I feel terribly sick,' but didn't look it, so I carried on.

'Now, it takes fifteen *mesures* to make what we call a *motte*, which is the amount you have to have before the mill will press it, so that if we have 60,000 olives per *mesure* that means that each *motte* is composed of – half a sec –

900,000 olives, every one of which we have picked up by hand. Think of it. 900,000 olives. 1,2,3,4,5—'

'I've simply got to have another drink—'

I got him one – 1 – and resupplied the others, counting 1,2,3,4, and one – 1 – for myself. I didn't count sitting down this time, because I wanted to get on with it.

'We, on the other hand, have collected in the last three – 1,2,3 – months fifty-five *mesures*. I could count them for you,' I said, 'if it would help you to picture the number more clearly—'

Someone shouted, very loudly, 'Stop it!' and then subsided, looking foolish, having let his nerve go like that.

'So then' I said, 'if we have gathered, olive by olive, in the last three – 1,2,3 – months no less than fifty-five *mesures* and there are 900,000 – dammit, call it 1,000,000 – olives in each *mesure* that means we have personally picked up, individually and by hand, the spanking total of 55,000,000 olives, put them into sacks and taken them down to the mill.'

Someone said, 'Without counting, just giving it to us in round figures, how much olive oil is that?'

'We've approximately,' I said, 'and allowing for mathematical error, round about one hundred and fifty litres of oil or, in British measurement thirty-three gallons.'

'Good Lord. What are you going to do with it all?'

With all the counting I'd been doing this hadn't occurred to me.

'I suppose,' I said, 'just use if for salad dressing.' But I was already counting their ears, the pictures on the walls and the panes in the french windows.

Nasty expectations

In the interests of giving me a few more trembling years on earth a plan arose 'to get someone in to do it for me', and as soon as possible, the reference being to the cutting of the grass.

Our very own grass. The four modestly sized lawns that are not so much lawns as rough carpets made of tightly knotted strands of dandelion, daisy, clover, bindweed, scutch grass, butch grass and often mouldering moss.

I've worn out three lawnmowers on this stuff, whirling around twice a week in two and a half hours dead, in and out of the bushes, round and round the trees, up and down the bit with the flat stones in it, except that four of them aren't all that flat and if mown chew up the machine in a single screaming second.

And now someone was coming in to do it for me, an impertinence on a level with our domestic lady cleaning my teeth, in my face. Or some old man walking four miles every morning to give me a helping hand in taking the top off my breakfast boiled egg. Of all the supererogatory sections—

Not knowing, exactly, what 'supererogatory' meant I stopped at this point. Madame snapped up the opportunity to telephone a man highly recommended for his lawnmowing technique and they made a firm rendezvous for 9 a.m. in a week's time, giving me a full seven days in which to contemplate the appalling future.

I knew what was going to happen. For some inconceivable reason I was not going to be in the garden, or anywhere near it, at 9 a.m. the following Tuesday, leaving my holy lawnmower exposed to barbarous assault, subsequently to be driven into reducing the whole garden to a sea of mud.

No one else knows a single thing about another man's lawnmower. He knows nothing about the essential tickling, soothing, smoothing and then the sudden jerk that brings her to roaring life. A man trying to start someone else's lawnmower relies upon a seven pound hammer as the only necessary tool.

For a while I thought about giving him written instructions, to be left conspicuously on the machine, and without delay saw that a mere week would be far too short a period of time in which to produce two quarto-sized pages, single spacing, in the French language and probably uselessly, at that, seeing that he would almost certainly be versed only in Italian, Spanish, Greek or some Bulgarian *patois*.

It was bad enough to think about what he would do to my machine to get it going, but a million times worse to picture what would happen after he had.

For instance, buried in our weed lawns in the most unexpected places, are miniature fountains from which water is sprayed by a powerful pump, an invaluable device in the heat of the summer. But quite a lot of these little fountains stick up an inch or two above the ground, just at the right height to get their heads lopped off by a lawnmower. They are beautiful pieces of precision-turned bronze that can strip the blade from a mower in a single flash, at the same time doing fatal damage to the machine itself. So that will be one new lawnmower and five or six new fountains, currently priced at about £30 each. A good day's work.

Of course, it would be a good idea to put flower pots over them, but he'd be sure to begin by removing all the flower pots, on the grounds that they were in his way, and forget where they'd been to begin with, with the result that—

It was too awful to think about, so I tried to think about something else – and came up with a beauty. The flex, quivering with electricity, that runs along the bottom of the hedge and then plunges underground, subsequently to climb to the lights in the trees beside the *boule* court. One touch of the lawnmower on that lot and an instant explosion, a sheet of flame and a carbonized lawnmowing expert, with hundreds of relatives clamouring for compensation.

What actually happened, when he arrived on the Tuesday, with two young men, was beyond belief. He made some adjustments to my mower, started it with a subtle flick of the wrist and it purred more beautifully than ever. He left, saying he would return at 4.30 p.m. and the two young men got on with the job, one with the mower and the other with the long-handled shears. They did it simply superbly. No fountain lopping, no explosions, no paving stone chewing and every edge meticulously neat. Then they spread fertilizer, highly scientifically, and watered every crumb of it in, with the hose.

If only they'd said, in advance, how good they were going to be, they would have saved me from a singularly nasty week.

At Life's Door

Rubber bone time

'Oh, and by the way,' I said, finishing off Doctor's report, 'he said it would do me no harm to have an occasional walk.'

In fact, Doctor had said I should take a walk *every* day, to regenerate my circulation, and went into even further detail. Stout shoes, loose, warm clothing and no walking up steep hills into east winds.

I understood the wisdom of the last injunction but became confused when he went on to the speed and duration of the exercise, becoming somewhat woolly himself.

'I don't want you to try breaking any records,' he said, without specifying which ones. 'Just do it in your own time annd stop when you've had enough.'

I asked him how I was supposed to get back, hoping to lead him so far from his original suggestion that he – and I – would forget all about it. He outmanoeuvred me, however, by showing me to the door with the news that he had another patient waiting, leaving the whole matter so loose and inconclusive that I thought nothing of reporting it to Madame. A fatal move.

'An occasional walk?' she said. 'But surely every day. Just have a nice little walk.'

I'd stepped straight into a man-trap and started thrashing about.

'A nice little walk?' I tried a sigh and a sneer at the same time. 'Tell me – what's "nice" about walking? How little is "a little walk"?'

The theme seemed to be going well so I expanded it.

'Let us get our definitions quite clear,' I said. 'At what speed, for instance, is this activity to be conducted? At what period of the day or night and for what duration? Or am I supposed to be breaking records—?'

I realized I'd got back into approximately the same losing situation I'd been in with Doctor, so I broke out into new ground.

'I should very much like to know,' I said, 'the name, address and physical condition of anyone who ever got cured of anything by walking. It's probably dangerous. I bet you walking has killed or permanently maimed millions of people, expelled from the security of their homes on to pitted roads beset by slavering wild dogs—'

'I'll take you for a nice little walk,' Madame said, 'when the rain stops.'

'With my leash – or a rubber bone – in my mouth?' But Madame had gone, unable to take any more of this pitiless scorn, leaving me alone to savour the details of my sentence. To wit: taking a walk, preferably brisk, every day, to restore the heart and circulation, both of which seemed to me to be in prime condition, if left alone.

Walking. Of all the pointless activities known to man. Just walking there, wherever it was, and then coming back again, with nothing whatever to do, during the procedure, except to fight off boredom. And pain?

I know how to walk. I've walked thousands of miles along the fairways – and rather more in the rough – of countless golf-courses, not even aware of the fact that I'm walking, being preoccupied with the problems of getting the ball on to the distant green in one or, at the very most, four more shots. I've even walked in cities, distances as great as two hundred yards, having been compelled to leave the car, by law, in prescribed parking areas. But walking, just for walking's sake? And particularly around here, because of the old people's home in such close proximity.

Twice a day four or five of them – either solo or duo – struggle up the slight slope of the lane that passes our house, turn at the crossroads at the top and fly – relatively speaking – back down the hill again. If and when this walking business breaks out I can tell you one thing that isn't going to happen. I'm not going to be ploughing *up* the hill when these leathery oldsters are skating down it, particularly as one of them wants me to write his biography. On innumerable occasions, catching me opening the garage doors, he's sketched in the gravamen of his life; i.e. eleven days of it, gallantly given to *la belle rance* at Verdun, rewarded during the Second World War by denunciation by his mother-in-law to the Gestapo, for reasons as yet undisclosed. I'm certainly not going to be nailed by him, coming down full of air while I'm struggling up, holding on to low walls and bushes, trying to catch an errant breath.

The other trouble around here is that two possible 'nice walks' terminate in jungly *culs-de-sac*, so that when you've got there the only place you can go to is back. There are no bars, restaurants or single ladies under forty to call upon *en route* or at any of the three termini. Nor can a taxi be summoned except by prearranged smoke signals . . .

It was in this way that I spent the next couple of days in search of more and more nails to bang into the walker's coffin until suddenly I lost the biggest and best one. The rain, which most unfairly stopped.

'Lucky doggy,' said Madame. 'Beautiful weather. Just nice for walky-walkies. Don't get into any fights.' And shut the front door on my muzzle.

I started off down the road at no great speed to be accosted, at the crossroads, by the red-haired bitch, the one that hangs around there every evening about six, prime soliciting time. Not that she made an overt proposal, but merely sauntered ahead of me down the lane, demonstrating a most unusual action of the hips. Then, for some apparently artless reason, she turned sideways, pausing for a moment, and I saw she, too, was a dog, one of the gang that get together several times a day for a really good barking, which continues until they get sore throats or find something fractionally better to do.

I knew this lurcher was a member of the barking gang because he had the aimless, unemployable, scatterbrained look of all the others, the mob who trot around all day looking for something to do, giving the unmistakable impression that when they find it it won't take them more than a couple of minutes to do it and when they've finished they won't know what they've done. To show, then, that they're really with it they have another barking session so frantic as to suggest a dog fight in which at least two or three of them will lose their lives.

These creatures all wear shabby leather collars, indicating that they've all got some kind of homes of their own – homes outside or inside which they should be sitting, to my mind, all day and all night long, in silent guardianship, instead of galloping about frightening birds, babies and worms in a perpetual, mindless motion, accompanied by barking that shatters the mind.

This dog, however, seemed to have a roughly prepared plan to accompany me on my walk, the possibly two and a half miles up hill and down dale circuit through the rock-strewn scrubland, dotted with feeble oaks and diseased pines, that constitutes our share of the Provençal *maquis*. He trotted ahead of me, giving me – perhaps intentionally – a clear view of the action of his back legs. In a curious way he looked like two dogs put together, the back legs being on a different plane to the front ones, so that he proceeded, athletically, in a crab-like way, like a small car with a bent chassis.

Striding out after this animal, swinging my stout cane, I felt just like a man going for a bracing walk with his faithful dog, Rover – an almost moving image, apart from two deficiencies. The stout cane was, in fact, a putter, purchased from Fred Smith, Royal Dublin professional and club-maker, in June, 1931, but now in the discards, seeing that in the past forty-eight years it had never learned the trick of slotting in the vital seven-footer, with a one and a half inch swing from the left, and for its trouble now had its blade wrapped in an old strip of towel bound with green sticky tape, providing an upholstered grip, with the original grip down below, seeking its way amid the stones. Not so much a stout cane, more a home-made bodge-up.

Nor did I know the dog's name. For years I've been calling all dogs Rover, irrespective of their given names like – all too like – Poggles, Sniffy, Maxie and Gwen. 'Rover' is as far as I want to get into intimacy with any dog ever whelped, so now I let out a ringing cry, '*Rhovair – veins içi!*'

The dog actually stopped, but without looking round. He's got the '*Viens içi*' bit, but '*Rhovair*' must have told him I'd been shouting at somebody else. After a moment he resumed his crab-like trot, leading the way to wherever we might be going.

At the old ruin on top of the hill we turned left, down the rocky, brambley path that leads to the track which has been scooped out of the jungle by fire engines, looking for the heart of forest fires, and now – with seeming courtesy – Rhovair yielded the lead to me. He was close on my heels as we made our way downhill, so close, indeed, that I began to think he might be contemplating assault upon my person from the rear. I turned, with the intention of reading his mind, if any. Instantly, he cowered away, certain I was going to beat his brains out with my putter. We resumed our process, in the same order as before, both trying to repair our faces.

After the fire-break, on the path that leads up to the entrance to the Château Poniatowski, Rhovair took the lead again, this time with the engaging addition of waiting for me around every corner, with a look that said, explicitly, 'Whoever that huge blue and white thing belongs to I hope it knows where we are, because I'm far off my beat.' The moment he saw me coming he went trotting on again, happily sideways, but the moment he reached the road he was off like a bullet down the hill and was deep into a jam session with his unspeakable friends by the time I got home, tearing the air apart outside our kitchen window on their No. 1 barking ground.

I must admit, the following evening, that it was I who did the loitering at the crossroads, but my new – well, friend – failed to show up, probably having forgotten all about me or not even remembering what had happened to him the day before.

A pity, really. I'd come to think of him as – Brownie.

Now I do my walks all alone, under the hated name of – Rover.

Little Kiss and Dr Merlin

Many of us have been manipulated in our time.

I don't mean manipulated in the sense of being taken for a ride by evil financiers, or used for their own ends by scheming women. I mean worked upon by other people's hands, so that we may be relieved – if only for the moment – of all those knots, nodules, lesions, adhesions, compactions, infractions, tensions and just plain agonies of the bones and the muscles and all the other working parts –

some of them only just – that seem to afflict so many of us during the whole of our brave little lives.

Much mystery is attached to manipulation, be it massage or the one where the operative takes your head between his mighty hands and screws your neck so that you're looking over your left shoulder blade at one moment and peering dizzily over the right a second later.

The mystery lies in the fact that the manipulator or masseur who takes over from the last one is always absolutely certain that his predecessor has got it all wrong, and that instead of working upon what this dangerous incompetent considered to be an impacted fibula tibula he should have been kneading away, or wrenching at, your misplaced ursus major.

For instance, I once had a man who put me into a plaster-of-paris barrel, on the grounds that only total immobilization of the spine would save me, within weeks, from a lifetime in a bathchair. To save his good suit he put on a rubber apron that covered him from the neck to the ground, preparatory to covering me and the walls of our bedroom with plaster-of-paris. Within weeks I was not in a bathchair but in this barrel, which had become so loose that I had to hold up the lower edges of it whilst taking the shortest of promenades.

One day I stepped out of it and bent, for

some medical reason, double, went to call upon the most marvellous old man around the corner who had the most wonderful hands. (Thus do we speak of our saviours.)

I told him about the barrel and he said, 'That must have kept you warm during the winter, but it wouldn't have done anything else.'

He then tied my arms together in a clove-hitch, sheep-shanked my legs, bore down upon me with the weight of an elephant, grunted, wrenched, all the knots flew apart and I stood upright for the first time in a month. He advised me to play thirty-six holes of golf at once and if I found myself in pain at the end of it to play thirty-six more the following day. The treatment worked perfectly.

Some years later I bent down to pick up a pin, for luck, and felt that tiny, piercing, split-second tweaking of some nerve or other that means the back has 'gone out' again. Bent double once more, and this time driven to a borrowed walking-stick to get round to the premises of a fully qualified bone-man who had performed absolute miracles upon several friends. The previous wonderful old man had died; from over-exertion.

The new man had a lot of X-ray pictures taken, found some degenerative changes in, I think, the osteophytical apophysealatic verte-brae, offered to mend them with the knife, accepted my refusal with good humour and gave me a short course of massage which enabled me at least to get rid of the walking-stick.

In the following years I let my back go in and out as it liked, preferring not to clutter it with too many divergent diagnoses and treatments, until suddenly, the other day, I got it in the neck.

Back well in but the neck absolutely rigid, revealing itself to my tentative fingers to be a mass of knots and nodules and lesions and adhesions as iron-hard as the rivets in a battleship. Also, any attempt to turn it produced a sound like gravel being decanted from a lorry.

It was all I could do to get to the airport to meet our two dear friends from Bangkok, mother and daughter, both of them exquisite, tiny Thai-size. As we drove home up the hill I felt two minute Thai hands on the back of my neck, exploring like feathers. I looked in the driving-mirror. It was the daughter, whose name in English means – so lovely I can barely bear to write it down – Little Kiss. Little Kiss nodded back and wriggled her super-slender fingers, seeming to promise super-massage to come.

It came, three times a day for the next five days, miniscule, probing fingers, searching out every nodule, shooting every burning knot, on and on, until I dissolved into a state of total Buddhist bliss.

On the day before they left, after swimming, Little Kiss suggested I lie face-down beside the pool. A moment later I felt tiny, searching feet squirming up and down my apophysealactic vertebrae. Little Kiss, going for a walk from coccyx to neck and back again and O Nirvana – O Arcadia – O Simple Ecstasy – as she did so she was nonchalantly nibbling at a peach. Match that against a plaster barrel!

For some time after that I – unlike Little Kiss – seemed to be walking on air, almost upright, almost dancing indeed at the relief from the grindings in the back that are built into the human frame by the convention that compels us to hobble about on our back legs rather than sprint around on all-fours until the day came – the inevitable day – when everything got much worse.

It was obvious that Little Kiss's foot and finger fairy treatment could be blamed in no way for this relapse – that kind of thing can only do good – but on the other hand Little Kiss was home in Bangkok and I was in agony, with the additional and very serious symptom of a rigidity of both elbows which meant that either or both of them could be raised only by gritting the teeth, with a lot of splashing of refreshment to follow.

It was this emergency that led me to take the whole lot to Dr Merlin, who had been highly recommended by a friend. That, of course, is not his real name, but if ever there was a magic medico it is he, built like a rock at the age of eighty-five, with hands like a pair of pliers if he finds pressure of that kind to be a necessity, although as an acupuncturist he really works with short steel pins.

I told Dr Merlin first about the red-hot rocks that had taken the place of muscles in my right shoulder and neck. He gave me a touch of the pliers on the *left* hand side. I rose vertically from the chair with a cry which rattled the windows. As though kneading dough he began to work swiftly on the rocks on both sides, sticking in pins, imperceptibly, as he ground away. Within a minute or two the rocks had become as soft and supple as they must have been when I was only fwee!

'Now lie down on the couch,' said Dr Merlin. 'You've obviously got long legs.'

With my head and shoulders all lovely and light and airy I nonetheless stiffened. I thought he was going to shorten my legs so that I'd come out as a man of about five feet two.

But he had said, 'You've obviously got a longer leg,' and I had. My left leg – a malaise well known to the magician – was exactly two inches longer than the right one. Some more pummeling, pounding and pricking and, as swiftly as the rock-reduction, both my legs were the same length.

'Stand up,' said Dr Merlin. I did so. He said, 'That's nice,' and pointed out that my shoulders were now at the same level.

I told him I had been sure for thirty years

that my right shoulder had dropped through a surfeit of slashing at golf balls in heavy rough, a deformity noticeable in even professional golfers. 'Your pelvis has been canted,' said Dr Merlin, 'not your shoulder. Lie down again.'

He armed himself with a small wooden bowl filled with what looked like rather dirty cottonwool. He set it alight. It smoked thinly. He passed it up and down my back, releasing muscles that had felt like wire netting for years. I asked him the name of this curious instrument. 'It's nothing,' said Dr Merlin. 'Just burning wormwood. I don't know how it works, but it does.'

He showed me another trick, holding in his right hand a gold watch on a thin chain. With his hand immovable, the watch began to swing violently backwards and forwards. In his left hand it hung dead. I tried it myself. In my right hand it did nothing. In my left it swung very gently. 'It's the electricity in you that repels the gold,' said Dr Merlin.

I had four days of this miracle treatment and came out of it standing dead straight, very nearly pain free, and feeling myself to be seven feet in height. Said Dr Merlin, 'It will take you a little time to grow into your new shape.'

The technicalities of acupuncture, involving Yin, Yang and meridians, are beyond me.

I only know that it works.

If only Little Kiss were here and she was

not only a walking, peach-nibbling masseuse but also a needle-sticker into the bargain – a little kiss? – life would be a veritable pre-taste of Paradise.

Le phleu

It's not all that easy having 'flu in French.

To start with it, they don't call it something recognizable like *le* (or *la*) *phleu*, so that foreigners could be sure they had the right disease harrumpsch—

Pardon. That one was right into the middle of the typewriter and, furthermore, moistening I fear beyond repair Page One. I hope it dries before it tears. I hope my tears dry before—

Bear down on that fever, old hand. You can make it.

The trouble having 'flu in French is that they call it *la grippe* which, medically speaking, can only be what small boys get from eating too many green apples with their little stomachs are still churning in terror from the act of stealing them. But what small boys don't get from eating too many green apples are molten ball-bearings in place of eyes, stewed rhubarb in place of legs, both lungs burning like the Crystal Palace and a cough like trained seals calling for their lunch. And the French go on calling this probably fatal ailment *la grippe*, causing me to believe that in addition to the foregoing symptoms I also have a severe stomach ache that comes from eating too many green apples which I have stolen in too much of a hurry HARRAAASCH—

Now that *éternuement*, or sneeze, has covered my glasses so that in addition to everything else I'm temporarily blind.

Imagine calling a sneeze an *éternuement*. It sounds like someone's getting interred, or buried, which wouldn't surprise me.

Send for Doctor Dupont. And when Dr Dupont gets here lock, with the speed of lightning, the door of the sickroom on the outside, because otherwise he'll have examined, diagnosed, prescribed and left before I have time to tell him about rhubarb leg.

Dr Dupont comes from the north of France and is therefore impatient of the more leisurely ways of us southerners. Dr Dupont, coming from the North, believes if he lets us intrude into the conversation a word of more than one syllable that he's going to be stuck with us for the rest of the day, and he hasn't time, seeing that everyone south of Lyon has *la grippe* and while he doesn't really mind missing lunch he would like to be home for dinner. . .

Whoossh!

That isn't another *éternuement*. That was

Dr Dupont, coming, prescribing and going. And *ma foi, parbleu et zut*, among the other prescriptions he's left one for six injections – *piqûres*, which can also mean stitching, quilting or wormholes. And if you think you were in trouble *before* Dr Dupont prescribed six wormholes *after* he's done so you've got more trouble than you can imagine could ever exist in the world, because now Madame has to run all the way down the hill to the chemist there to purchase at prohibitive cost the stuff I'm to be punctured with and then run up the hill again and then try to track down the *infirmière*, or the infirmary lady or district nurse on the telephone and she's *always* out, boring wormholes in somebody else, because she's the only one for miles around who is allowed to do it.

However, while we're waiting for the infirmary lady we can proceed with other aspects of the treatment because Madame has brought back a bottle of cough mixture, some yellow tablets and some white, maggot-like tubes, all for immediate consumption on the premises. And if I thought I had a touch of *le phleu* before the arrival of Dr Dupont I now believe I should be dissected without a second's delay on the grounds that what I've got could illuminate every single one of the dark places that medical science has been trying to get at for years.

The cough mixture is called *Sirop de Marrubène à la Codéthyline*, to which the great *phytothérapeute* Henry Leclerc has consecrated much study.

The yellow pills are called *Stafytracine* (*Virginiamycine-Tétracycline*) and they are active against most of the *cocci Gram-positif* and the *cocci Gram-négatif* but, as you can imagine, I don't give a damn about either of the *coccis*. I want to know about this *Virginiamycine*, which sounds to me as though the speedy Dr Dupont must be trying his hand at another branch of medicine altogether – i.e. gynaecology.

Even the larger *Larousse* dictionary, of course, makes no mention of *Virginiamycine*, touching only upon *Virginité*, which is one of the very few things I haven't got, so I pass on to the study of the literature concerning the white maggots.

They, apparently, are *Ultra-Levure Gelules Lyophilisée*, and have a remarkable power of proliferation. This seems to be the worst news yet, in that I know *levure* means yeast. I've been given tons of proliferating yeast for suspected virginity, with the great *phytothérapeute* Henry Leclerc lying in wait to lubricate the whole process with his sinister *Sirop de Marrubène*.

I wish to God I had a simple English cold.

God save the happy nuns

Citizen, not yet a Patient, rises early in Manchester Hotel facing with a smile, and back teeth locked together, another exciting British winter day, full of challenge, adventure and not a gleam of hope.

Cannot return to France, because French are having one-day national strike. Intention to hole up for twenty-four hours in one of multitudinous hotels round London Airport, if the building be completed in time and if British Airways have enough kerosene to transport body and, furthermore, if on arrival hotel bus has enough petrol to perform same service, always providing that on arrival at hotel hotel has enough electricity to provide lunch and a reading light and some minimal heating; if hotel is open for business at all.

At general prospect, plus imminent arrival of Christmas, Citizen grinds back teeth down to bone and immediately left ear becomes blocked, as does left nostril plus trembling and instability in right arm and leg and strewth my God Patient's had a stroke. Lightning, self-diagnosis. Poor, poor Patient.

Poor, poor me. So, comparatively, young, to go. What a bitter, bitter shame . . .

Patient, shaking, picks up phone to summon doctor, stretcher, ambulance, hearse, last rites (C. of E. please) and the Final Trumpet sounds. A hell bell. An hysterical, demented clanging, on and on and on. So the Last Trump is a Universal Police Car. Wouldn't you know it? Bell suddenly stops and Patient remembers last night's warning about fire drill 10.30 a.m. and apologies for any inconvenience caused. INCONVENIENCE!

Doctor arrives, diagnoses inflammation of inner ear, advises later flight to London, prescribes, puts out flipper for £4, has no change and leaves with a fiver. Phone call reveals all flights to London fully booked, if they go at all, trains very doubtful, happy Christmas.

Loyal hotel porter rushes out into heavy rain to fulfil prescription, kept waiting half an hour for three pills, Patient sitting trembling in car when Loyal comes galloping back and Manchester Airport going round and round in circles when Patient arrives.

Patient, leg dragging, makes his way down endless greenhouse to Gate 24 in company of eleven pint-sized, exuberant foreigners going home for Christmas yelping at one another possibly in Portuguese. Airport increases its revolutions, going into reverse and then suddenly up and down at unpredictable moments. Patient being searched by Securicor guards when, without warning, Patient's entire breakfast regains open air, the recoil throwing Patient to the ground. The more quickly moving guards and passengers avoid the worst of it. Rough but kindly hands, wheel chair, stretcher, ambulance, Patient left balancing narrow bed in airport infirmary with bed scraping its legs on ceiling, before sliding down walls, before going up again. Patient fills in time, once every ten minutes, with involuntary breakfast returning action, but well now dry but makes no difference. Poor, poor Patient. Goodbye, goodbye . . .

Patient finds himself fully clothed in hospital bed with fresh-faced, happy nun bending over him. Fresh-faced happy shoots in a bicycle pump-full of injection but Patient spends rest of night on non-existent breakfast delivery service, remaining wide awake for the purpose. In the morning extremely intelligent, charming doctor diagnoses 'small basilar artery branch thrombosis from which he is making an excellent recovery'.

Patient excellently recovered by following morning when Madame and Son enter presumed death chamber. They've been busy. Madame has arrived from Nice, Son from Paris. Madame has cancelled all Christmas preparations in France, found luxurious London flat in which Patient, if still living, can enjoy Christmas here, also arranged for car to make journey from London to Manchester and return and Son has Patient's dressing-gown in his suitcase. Patient bursts into tears.

Patient spends much of subsequent week fending off fresh-faced happy nuns who keep urging strong drink on him on grounds it will make him feel better. Patient refuses, guarding sanctity of his basilar artery, until final evening when he yields, happy nun pours him a roaster and he feels FINE. Madame arrives with car, Patient slotted into luxury flat in London and following morning into premises of Harley street neurologist who takes one look at relevant documents, one look at patient, and says, 'You've had a fairly severe migraine attack. Help yourself to a cigar, bottle of what you fancy, and have a happy Christmas.'

Madame, summoned from waiting-room, first almost faints, then goes off into peal after peal of laughter so uncontrolled that her vision is obscured by tears.

That's why we've come to London for the coal strike, the electricity cuts, the rail go-slow and the IRA bombings. Because of fuel rationing we cannot get a flight to Nice until next Sunday.

When she thinks I'm not watching her Madame's pretty shoulders still shake, and once again her eyes become veiled with moisture.

I'm going to give her a big, big cracker, for a very, very happy Christmas.

All down on one side

Well, anyway, the suffering Britons haven't had it so good for a long, long time.

It's almost sheer, blind good luck that Christmas should have fallen on a Saturday last year, spreading its beneficial waves not only backwards but also forwards, so that the most dedicated boiler scraper could take a whole month's holiday with a highly polished conscience, with a quietly convalescent fortnight to follow as he eased himself back into the rigours of industrial dispute or, in the case of some malcontents, actual toil. And, of course, the more sophisticated among these elements – the ones who keep a sharp eye on the outside world – knew that they had yet another bonus to which they could look forward, a gift from God arriving so quickly after the Christmas present that they had almost too little time to unwind after working to unwrap the new goodies with a steady hand. To wit, Easter falling, with an immense splash, right into the middle of yet another weekend.

A piece of paper, a stub of pencil and the simplest of calendars were the only tools required to dig out the exhilarating information that since Good Friday would be a holiday there would be little point in applying oneself to the looms or the lathes on the even better Thursday that preceded it, on the grounds that more than probably one would be entirely alone in the place of work, the reasoning here being that since Easter Monday would be still another well-deserved holiday it would be a matter of plain duty to get into good holidaying form before the whole festival broke out. Furthermore, only some daft old lad who had been banging away with the same hammer for about half a century would be soppy enough to turn up for ear-splitting labour on the following Tuesday, a day so deeply into the week that there would be little point in clocking in until the coming Monday, seeing that the factory would be scarcely even aired by then. The additional, incontrovertible fact that Easter nearly always falls on a weekend seems to be irrelevant to the planning in hand. As it seems to us oldsters, some of us semi-retired and the others so profoundly retired that not even heavy shelling could winkle them out of their bunkers. Why, right down here in the South of France all of us senior citizens, with almost nothing whatever to do either commercially or professionally, have become so excited by the Easter holidays that we've been grooving away at it virtually since 1 April, with at least a couple of weeks, when it's officially over, still to come.

For us, it's a matter of keeping up with the workers, people who go to places of work for fixed (loosely) hours for no less than five days per week. We feel it's up to us to show them that we, who have long since forgotten what the inside of an office or the most comfortable factory looks like, can relax from doing nothing with an abandon which they, toil-worn as they may be, can scarcely match.

Not that we, in the gallant sixties, are stone idle in our Easter pleasures. We are much concerned about one another's health, an occupation as demanding as putting doors, back to front, on motor-cars, on an assembly line which, for many complex reasons, has not been moving for the last three months.

When we meet we say, like veritable machines, 'Hello, how *are* you?' having already made a pretty accurate estimate, with data computerized, input of increasing weight, pallor, neck thinning, unusual blotches, all that kind of thing, but at least it gets the conversation going with a swing, all parties concerned with a very real interest in the contents.

'How am I? Well, to tell you the truth, I've got it all down the back of the leg again.'

'Oh, *no!*'

'Started early on Wednesday morning. Took a good dollop of biomicrostetholene, with the usual result that I got this damned rash.'

'You're getting a rash from biomicro? That's funny. It leaves me as breathless as a stranded—'

'Whale?'

'No, no. Just a *bit* breathless. It really gets me in the back of the neck. Starts round about the collar-bone, goes all round the back and comes out just below the other one. I've also got a touch of numbness in—'

'The brain?'

'Just the left hand side. But it's really more in the foot.'

We've actually had a brilliant young worker relaxing with us for Easter. He's hardly been able to get in a word about his craft of advertising because I've got it all over again, right here in the middle of the back.

X-rays on a hairpin bend

What a happy, sunny, smiling day it was last Tuesday, in my happy, smiling life.

All I had to do was to go to Grasse for an X-ray for this pain in the neck and on the way home pick up some anti-rust paint, if possible black *and* white – minor activities that could be carried out by a fairly well trained monkey – in any other city in the world.

I have no doubt that the Mayor of Grasse loves his perfumed city. I am perfectly certain that there are thousands of people who have lived in Grasse all their lives, and would not dream of leaving it for a single second. It is beyond question that millions of tourists have the happiest memories of this ancient and historic town and wouldn't half mind seeing it again.

I cannot understand any of this. Rather than go to Grasse for an X-ray and pick up some black and white anti-rust paint on the way home I would prefer to live for the rest of my existence in Pontyprid, with the wrong woman and a peevish mongrel dog. Any old time, because if you get into Grasse with a car you're in for hell-fire, mental torture, physical assault and probable arrest.

Grasse is built on the side of a cliff, so that all the exceedingly narrow streets are made of hairpin bends. There is a three-storey car-park hacked out of this cliff into which, if there be space available, your car fits as tightly as a finger into a glove, and in equal obscurity. In my time, in there, I have demolished a very small Fiat and a chariot filled to the brim with bottles, eggs and a ton of mixed vegetables, in the same manoeuvre.

Picture my pleasure, then, upon entering Grasse for this X-ray appointment, to find that the whole city was being dug up, so that all the hairpin bends up the face of the cliff were choked with immovable traffic. I got somewhere near the site of the X-ray factory at 10 a.m. – the precise time of my appointment – to find that the car-park I was aiming at – the only flat space for miles – had been turned into a taxi-rank. Roared at by enraged taxi drivers I concealed my car among theirs, and started running, looking for the X-ray place, in tropical heat. I found it at 10.20, in a precipitous side street, one of the shabbiest buildings I'd ever seen. I was instantly slotted, by an angry girl, into a waiting-room as cheerful as a prison cell, and then everything stopped, except for my mind racing with excuse and explanation to the police, who would certainly have dragged my car away already, if the taxi-drivers hadn't personally demolished it.

At 10.45 I got X-rayed by a grey haired doctor who urged me to look up to Heaven, illustrating the required position by putting his hands together, in prayer, beneath his chin. When I did likewise he snapped, 'Without the hands, please. I am very busy.' After he had seen the snaps he wrote out a report on a piece of orange paper with the most extraordinary writing method I had ever seen. He seemed merely to put his pen on the paper and then draw it to the left with the other hand, producing voluminous scrawlings. It took him quite some time. In another prison cell a less angry girl typed it out, whilst speaking continuously on the telephone. It took her even longer. When I got back to my car, at 11.5, a policeman was leaning against it. By mercy of God he was the nice Grasse policeman – a contradiction in terms if ever there was one. 'If I was you, M'sieu,' he said, 'I'd get out of town as quickly as possible.' And actually saluted me. I got out of town so quickly that I forgot about the black and white anti-rust paint, and didn't care.

When I got home I looked at the grey haired doctor's report and was struck with sudden terror.

It began: '*Unco-discartrhoses étagées de C4 à DI—*'

It seemed to be just plain madness, or rotten typing. What the doctor appeared to have written must have been 'Uncodiscar-thorses'. But what were these cart-horses doing in here, in English, when he was X-raying me in French? Nor had the dictionary ever heard of the word, 'Unco'. Short, perhaps, for 'uncoordinated'? 'Unco-ordinated cart-horses', galloping up and down my back. There's French medicine for you. I left that diagnosis on one side, and proceeded to the next brainwave. '*Discrète antéposition de C4 sur C5—*'

A discreet before positioning of vertebrae C4 on C5. Surely that kind of thing would never give anyone a pain in the neck? Or at least not as quickly as the last line: '*Pincement de l'espace inter-odonto-atloidien et de l'inter-ligne atloaxoidien droit—*'

It sounded exactly as though I'd got some Aztec fever. But next day our doctor told me I'd *only* got severe arthritis.

I knew where I caught that.

Grasse.

Ruptured in shadow

'It was simply beyond the power of my mind to appreciate the situation in its entirety,' I said to this man, who appeared not to be listening with absolute attention.

'I mean,' I went on, 'really to grip the thing by its basics was beyond me. There was I, slashed by the surgeon's scalpel, unable to walk, sitting in a ground-floor flat in London, watching people walking up – and down – the street outside and each and every one of them sweltering in the molten sunshine. With me inside, in deep shadow.'

The man had a furtive glance at his wristwatch.

I raised my voice a little. 'I don't know if you know this about me,' I went on, 'but when it comes to sunshine I'm your true blue professional sun worshipper. In the way of sun worshipping I'm right up there with the heavyweights. Show me a ray of sunshine ten miles away up the face of a sheer cliff and I'll run to it in my bare feet.'

The man seemed to half cover the beginning of a yawn.

'Over broken glass,' I said. 'Just to get into that miniscule spot of sunshine ten miles away up the face of this sheer cliff. And there I was, slashed, unable to walk, sitting day after day in deep shadow, watching the whole population of London staggering by, holding on to railings for support in a blistering, delicious, suffocating heat wave. Do you know what I did?'

He seemed to pull his mind back from some remote speculation. 'No,' he said.

'I actually pulled the curtains,' I said, 'me, this heavyweight, all-time champion worshipper of the sun, because the glare from outside was so intense I couldn't watch people playing cricket on television, in blistering, lovely heat.'

I felt it was time to speed the narrative, to give it a fresh slant. 'So,' I said, 'in the end I got strong enough to proceed with small, delicate steps, to Gate 13 at London Airport, to go home to the South of France and really make up for a hundred lost years of sun worshipping time. Strict instructions, of course, from my lady wife not to make any weighty purchases from the duty-free booze shop, in case I ruptured myself again, but on the plane, not to break the habit of a lifetime, I bought a single bottle of whiskey, in a cardboard box. You're not going to believe the next bit.'

'I shall try,' said the man.

'It was heavily overcast at Nice Airport. Low, grey cloud, with the threat of rain. In the South of France, after a heat wave in London into which I had been unable to get. Low, grey cloud with the threat of rain in the South of France at the beginning of June, when one should have been able to cook an omelette *aux fines herbes* on the pavement. And in the airport building the bottle of duty-free whiskey fell from my shaking hands and smashed itself to pieces. Welcome home. If there had been a whole, intact bottle of whiskey, duty-free or otherwise, lying on the ground I should have been unable – thanks to the surgeon's slashing and hacking – to bend down and pick it up, so that all I could do was to step over the shattered remnants of the bottle and fall into the arms of those who were waiting to bear me home. On the way home it began to rain. By the time we got home it was coming down in torrents, mingled with occasional gusts of hail. In the South of France at the beginning of June . . .'

'I really ought to—' the man began.

'It poured for the whole of that afternoon, all night and it was still at it next morning, improving its performance by the minute, and showing every sign of continuing to do so, which it did.'

'I know,' the man said. 'I was here.'

'So there was I, the all-time heavyweight sun worshipping champion, instead of lying in state beside the pool in my sun worshipping knickers – there was I, fully dressed, once again trapped indoors, but this time, instead of watching a heat wave going on outside, just watching the rain, as though I were in Scunthorpe in November. Then a friend rang from London to tell me that one of the lesser gossip columnists on one of the lower London newspapers had an item to the effect that I'd been seen, "in my usual condition", breaking a bottle of whiskey all over Nice Airport and instead of getting out my portable dustpan and brush and sweeping it up had simply walked away, gravely inconveniencing every single other person on the premises, at the time. Some varlet, observing the scene and eager to make a couple of quid for himself. Ensuring me of a warm welcome home to the perishing South of France in drenching rain at the beginning of June. I simply don't know how I found the strength to—'

'I've got to find the strength,' said the man, in a loud voice, 'to go back to London now, to a possible general strike, to reeling inflation and national bankruptcy, and without doubt it will be pouring with rain.'

I stretched myself more comfortably beside the pool in the returned and firmly established sun.

'I most sincerely hope so,' I said.

The worst book in the world

Condemned to a week of 'taking it easy', 'getting the feet up', 'not overdoing it' and, the final torment, 'having a little nap in the afternoon', I armed myself rapidly and therefore haphazardly with six paperbacks at a bookstall at London Airport, every single one of them describing themselves as 'seething, scorching, shocking, fearless, perverted, spicy' and 'packed with red-hot clinical sex'.

This was not because I was looking for this kind of – ah – material with which to enliven my octogenarian – or it seemed – convalescence, but simply because no other form of literary pabulum, in the potentially limitless field of fiction, was on view.

Shelf after shelf of skiny paperbacks, almost all of them rosy and juicy with naked persons on the cover, with mixed all-in wrestling evidently all the rage. Curiously enough, however, none of the performers showed a competitive spirit, their bland, remote expressions suggesting that their major concern lay in the question of how much longer they'd have to go on posing, starkers, in this perishing cold studio before they could get home to a nourishing meat tea, knowing perfectly well, at the same time, that none of their current activities would illustrate any aspect of the plot inside.

I was glad to receive a small plastic bag from the bookstall lady in which to conceal my selections, until I could get them back to the privacy of home, because I can never find the right thing to do with my face whilst reading works of this kind in public. A stern, Puritan look can suggest a super-annuated sexual innocence, whilst an accelerated whipping through the pages, accompanied by a furtive licking of the lips, indicates that the reader could do with more healthy exercise and many, many more cold baths. Nor does there ever seem to be anything in between.

With my feet up, then, taking it easy, overdoing nothing, I stacked my miniature library beside me and began to read with sufficient care to ensure that the six books would last out the whole convalescent week. The first volume had a blank faced girl on the cover in a topless bikini, looking at a single yellow rose stuck in the barrel of a revolver as though she had never seen such an amazing contiguity before – understandably, really, in all conscience. I opened page one and found myself equally short. In a scant two hundred words we were knee-deep in dirty work in the unspeakable Middle East, so swiftly, indeed, that not even the CIA had had time to stick a rose in the spout of a gun. If, that is, they were the CIA and not the KGB or, perhaps, the Palestinian Liberation lads in equally adroit disguise. Weaving in and out of all this plotting and planning, for purposes as not yet revealed, was the standard British agent in the stained mackintosh left over from John le Carré backed, or about to be stabbed in the back, by the suave, silvery haired operator for the Foreign Office, the part that has been played for so many years by that lovely, wily old actor Willie Hyde White.

By the beginning of Chapter Two I was bogged down in total incomprehension, but still reading with finicky attention to make the proceedings in hand last out at least until dinner time, and dreading, as ever, the half-way mark. The slow climb uphill to this point can take up to two and a half hours, but after this it's helter-skelter down the slippery slope to the final paragraph which, in its endeavour to explain what has been going on, is often so irrelevant that it could well constitute the beginning of a whole new thriller, and probably will.

By Friday, with only two days to go, I was two-thirds of the way through Volume No. 5, the mind rotted with sensational, searing tosh, and with only one more to go – the story of an ugly young Polish girl, clearly visible on the cover through a transparent, crimson peignoir, on her way to becoming a New York model and subsequently a Holly-wood film star, a career shared by many another (previous) virgin during the past week's reading.

I was bold enough to embark upon this one, seeing that it was two inches thick and liable to last for about twenty-four hours, on Friday night and started, on Page One, as though I had sat on a nail. The first words were, 'Mercy frantically squealed her passionate enthusiasm'. To the suggestion, if you please, on the part of her gay protector that she should have a nose-bob. I advanced, gingerly, into this steaming jungle, unable to believe the evidence of my eyes. On page forty-nine Mercy, after removal of her bandages, finds, 'A new lower modish piteous throbbing voice, surprising after her operative nasality'. And on page fifty Mercy, complimented upon her appearance by a film producer, says, 'Your appreciation is appreciated', but says it with 'discrediting acidulousness'. And, instantly, 'An unsuccessfully suppressed snicker sneaked its way out of her'.

Thank God, I shall always have one book in hand in which I never even got to the halfway mark.